A LEXICOGRAPHICAL AND HIS-
TORICAL STUDY OF
ΔΙΑΘΗΚΗ

The Department of Biblical and Patristic Greek, of The University of Chicago, proposes to issue, from time to time, Historical and Linguistic Studies in Literature Related to the New Testament. These Studies will be grouped in three series: I, Texts; II, Linguistic and Exegetical Studies; III, Historical Studies. The volumes in each series will be issued in parts from time to time.

A LEXICOGRAPHICAL AND HISTORICAL STUDY OF *ΔΙΑΘΗΚΗ*

FROM THE EARLIEST TIMES TO THE END OF THE CLASSICAL PERIOD

BY

FREDERICK OWEN NORTON, Ph.D.

WIPF & STOCK · Eugene, Oregon

Wipf and Stock Publishers
199 W 8th Ave, Suite 3
Eugene, OR 97401

A Lexicographical and Historical Study of DIATHEKE from the
Earliest Times to the End of the Classical Period
By Norton, Frederick Owen
ISBN 13: 978-1-60608-512-7
Publication date 2/12/2009
Previously published by University of Chicago, 1908

PREFACE

The term διαθήκη is of special interest from two standpoints—that of the student of Greek law, and that of the student of the New Testament. Writers on Greek law have discussed the Greek will with varying degrees of completeness, but have failed to notice and account for the fact that the word used to designate it was also used to designate what might be called a solemn agreement or compact. Scholars have long been divided as to the meaning of this word in the New Testament, some claiming that it should invariably be translated "will" or "testament," and others that it always means "covenant;" while a third class of writers claim that in some instances it should be rendered "will" and in others "covenant." With reference to a passage in Paul's writings (Gal. 3:15) there is a threefold division among interpreters.[1]

As no special lexicographical work has been done on this word either in classical or in Hellenistic Greek, and the need of such work has been recognized by scholars, no apology is needed for the present dissertation, the purpose of which is to investigate the use of the term in Greek literature, from the earliest times in which it can be found, or in which there are traces of an institution that later came to be designated by it, through the classical period. As the primary object in undertaking this work was to make a contribution to New Testament study, it is hoped that it may form a basis for further investigation in Hellenistic literature.

In the lexicographical study the year 300 B. C. has been arbitrarily chosen as a limit to the investigation, the aim being simply to carry it well through the classical period. In the historical study no sharp line of demarkation is observed; but only in a few instances, for obvious reasons, has the ordinary imaginary boundary-line been overstepped.

In the course of the lexicographical study it was found that no English term carries with it the exact connotation of διαθήκη, and that its technical use in Greek law did not correspond with accuracy to our terms "will" and "testament." Accordingly, in order to bring out its

---

[1] "Testament:" The Vulgate, Luther, Erasmus, Olshausen, etc.; "covenant" (*Bund*): Jerome, Beza, Calvin, Flatt, Hilgenfeld, Meyer, Lightfoot, etc.; "Determination" or "ordainment" (*Bestimmung, Willensfügung*): Matthias, Lipsius, Hoffmann, Schott, etc.

essential signification and the relation of its phases of development, it was necessary to investigate the origin and development and essential character of the institution which it was chiefly used to designate. From this necessity arose the second part of the dissertation, the aim of which is not to give an exhaustive treatment of the Greek will, but to discuss that institution only in so far as it is necessary in order to understand the term from a lexicographical standpoint, and to show its essential connotation.

The sources for this investigation are specifically indicated by the usual abbreviations, in the notes, which contain also references to modern writings which I have found helpful in the way of suggestion or comparison. I subjoin a list of books and articles consulted.

To Professor Ernest D. Burton, head of the Department of Biblical and Patristic Greek in The University of Chicago, who suggested the need of this investigation, and to whose faithful and inspiring instruction I am indebted more than I can tell, I wish to express my deep and abiding gratitude.

TABLE OF CONTENTS

BIBLIOGRAPHY

Annuaire de l'association pour l'encouragement des études grecques. Paris, 1868–87.

BARILLEAU, Des sources de droit grec. Paris, 1883.

BEAUCHET, Histoire du droit privé de la république athénienne; 3 vols. Paris, 1897.

BECKER, Charikles. Berlin, 1877.

BOECKH, Corpus inscriptionum Graecarum. Berlin, 1828–77.

BONNER, Evidence in Athenian Courts. Chicago, 1905.

BRUNS, Die Testamente der griechischen Philosophen. In Zeitschrift der Savigny-Stiftung für Rechtsgeschichte, Vol. I, Romanistische Abtheilung, I, pp. 1–53.

BRUNS UND SACHAU, Ein syrisch-römisches Rechtsbuch aus dem fünften Jahrhundert. Leipzig, 1880.

BÜCHERLER UND ZITELMANN, Das Recht von Gortyn. Frankfurt am Main, 1885.

BUNSEN, De iure hereditario Atheniensium. Göttingen, 1813.

BURY, A History of Greece, to the Death of Alexander the Great. London, 1890.

CAILLEMER, Le droit de tester. In Annuaire des études grecques, 1870.

CAUER, Dilectus inscriptionum Graecarum. Leipzig, 1883.

CONRAT, Das Erbrecht im Galaterbrief. In Zeitschrift für die neutestamentliche Wissenschaft, Vol. V, 1904.

DARESTE, Les plaidoyers civiles de Demosthène; 2 vols. Paris, 1875.

Nouvelles études d'histoire du droit. Paris, 1902.

DARESTE, HAUSSOULIER and REINACH, Recueil des inscriptions juridiques. Paris, 1891–94 (*IJG.*).

DITTENBERGER, Sylloge inscriptionum Graecarum. Leipzig, 1883–1901.

FOUCART, Des associations religieuses chez les Grecs. Paris, 1873.

FUSTEL DE COULANGES, La cité antique: Paris, 1890.

Nouvelles recherches sur quelques problèmes d'histoire. Paris, 1891.

GANS, Das Erbrecht in weltgeschichtlicher Entwickelung; 3 vols. Berlin, 1824.

GIDE, Étude sur la condition privée de la femme. Paris, 1885.

GOLIGHER, Isaeus and Attic Law. In Hermathena, No. XXXII, Dublin, 1906.

GROTE, History of Greece; 12 vols.

GUIRAUD, La propriété foncière en Grèce jusqu' à la conquète romaine. Paris, 1893.

Du droit de succession chez les Athéniens. In Revue de législation, Vol. XVI, pp. 97 ff.

HATCH, Studies in Biblical Greek. Oxford, 1889.

HILLE, De testamentis in iure Attico. Amstelod, 1898.

HOFMANN, Beiträge zur Geschichte des griechischen und römischen Rechts. Vienna, 1870.

JANNET, Les institutions sociales et le droit civil à Sparte. Paris, 1880.

JEBB, The Attic Orators from Antiphon to Isaeus. London, 1893.

KENNEDY, The Orations of Demosthenes; 5 vols. London, 1863.

KENYON, Hypereides. London, 1893.

Aristotle on the Constitution of Athens. London, 1892.

LIGHTFOOT, Saint Paul's Epistle to the Galatians. London, 1890.

LOBECK, Aglaophamus; 2 vols. Königsberg, 1829.

MAINE, Ancient Law. London, 1891.

MEIER AND SCHÖMANN, Der attische Process; new edition by Lipsius. Berlin, 1883–87.

MERRIAM, Law Code of Cretan Gortyna. In American Journal of Archaeology, 1885, 1886.

MEYER, Kritisch-exegetischer Kommentar über das Neue Testament: Der Brief an die Galater; new edition by Sieffert. Göttingen, 1899.

MITTEIS, Reichsrecht und Volksrecht in den östlichen Provinzen des römischen Kaiserreichs. Leipzig, 1891.

MOY, Étude sur les plaidoyers d'Isée. Paris, 1876.

PERROT, Essais sur le droit public et privé de la république athénienne: Le droit public. Paris, 1867.

L'éloquence politique et judiciaire à Athènes. Paris, 1873.

PLATNER, Der Process und die Klagen bei den Attikern. Darmstadt, 1824, 1825.

RAMSAY, An Historical Commentary on Galatians. New York, 1900.

RIDDER, L'idée de la mort en Grèce à l'époque classique. Paris, 1897.

RIDGEWAY, The Early Age of Greece. Cambridge, 1901.

ROBERTS, Introduction to Greek Epigraphy. Cambridge, 1887.

ROBIOU, Questions de droit attique politique, administratif et privé. Paris, 1880.

ROEDER, Beiträge zur Erklärung und Kritik des Isaios. Jena, 1880.

ROSENMÜLLER, Dissertatio de vocabulo διαθήκη in Commentationes Theologicae, Vol. II. Leipzig, 1795.

SANDYS, Aristotle's Constitution of Athens. London, 1893.

SANDYS and PALEY, Select Private Orations of Demosthenes; 2 vols. Cambridge, 1896.

SCHMIEDEL, article "Galatea" in Encyclopaedia Biblica. New York, 1901.

SCHNEIDER, De iure hereditario Atheniensium. Munich, 1851.

SCHÖMANN, Isei Orationes xi. Greifswald, 1831.

SCHULIN, Das griechische Testament verglichen mit dem römischen. Basel, 1882.

SEIFERT, De iure hereditario Atheniensum. Greifswald, 1842.

TELFY, Corpus juris attici. Pesth, 1868.

THALHEIM in HERMANN, Lehrbuch der griechischen Antiquitäten; II, 1: Rechtsalterthümer. Freiburg i. B., 1895.

VINCENT, Word Studies in the New Testament. New York, 1900.

WYSE, The Speeches of Isaeus. Cambridge, 1904.

ZIEBARTH, article διαθήκη in Pauly's Real-Encyclopädie. 1903.

PART I
THE LEXICOGRAPHICAL STUDY

CHAPTER I

DERIVATION AND LITERAL MEANING

The noun διαθήκη is derived from the verb διατίθημι, which is composed of the preposition διά and the verb τίθημι.

διά is from the root δυ, whence also come δύο, δύω, δοί-οι, δι- (in comp.), *two;* δίς for δϝίς or δυίς, *twice;* δεύ-τερος for δϝέ-τερος, *second;* δοι-ή, *doubt;* δί-χα, δί-χθα, *in two;* δι-σσός, *double;* δί-πλοος, *twofold;* δυώ-δεκα, δώ-δεκα.

Skt. *duá, dvi-* (in comp.), "two;" *dvis* "twice;" *dva-jás,* "twofold;" *dui-tyas,* "second." Zd. *dva, bi-,* two; *bi-tya,* "second."

Lat. *duo, bi-* (for *dvi*), *bis* (for *duis*), *dis-, bi-ni.* Umbr. *du-r,* "two."

The fundamental idea is that of *duality.* That this is retained in composition may be seen from a comparison of the following meanings:

1. *From one side or end to the other, through,* as in διαβαίνω; *to the end, utterly,* as in διαμάχομαι, διαφθείρω, etc., and so to denote *pre-eminence,* as in διαπρέπω, διαφέρω, etc.

2. *In two, asunder, at variance,* as in διαιρέω, διαφωνέω, διαφέρω, etc.

3. *One with another,* of simple mutual relation, as in διαγωνίζομαι, διαεΐδω, διαφιλοτιμέομαι (all used with τινί).

4. *Between, in part,* as in διάλευκος, διάχρυσος, διάχλωρος, etc.

The root of τίθημι is θε- whence also come θέσις, *a placing, deposit, position;* θέμα, *a proposition;* θέσμος, *something set down* or *established,* a *rule;* θέμις, *a law established* by custom; θεμέλιον, foundation; θής, *a hired laborer,* θήκη, *a place for putting anything in, box, tomb, sheath;* θῆμα = θήκη.

Skt. *dhâ, da-dhâ-mi,* "place, lay, do;" *dhâ-man,* "dwelling-place, law, way, condition;" *dhâ-tr,* "creator;" *dhâ-tus,* "stuff." Zd. *dâ,* "place, make, produce;" *dâ-tam,* "creature;" *dâ-mi,* "creation." Lat. *facio.*

The radical meaning is to *put, place, set;* hence to *bring* a thing *into a place,* or *situation, bring about, cause.*

With the radical sense of τίθημι and διά in mind, the literal signification of διαθήκη can best be seen from a comparison of other compounds of διά; e. g.:

διάβασις, a *going from one* side or end *to the other*, a *crossing over to the other side*, Hdt. 1. 186; a *ford*, Thuc. 7. 74; a *bridge*, Xen. *Anab.* 2. 3. 10.

διαβόλη, a *throwing from one to another, slander*, Hdt. 3. 66. 73; a *quarrel* with someone, ἡ πρός τινα δ., Plut. 479 B; cf. διαβάλλω, to *make a quarrel between; ἐμὲ καὶ Ἀγάθωνα*, Plat. *Symp.* 222 C, D; δ. ἀλλήλοις, Arist. *Pol.* 5. 11. 8.

διάγγελος, a *secret messenger*, a *go-between*, Thuc. 7. 73.

διάγνωσις, a *distinguishing one* thing *from another*, a *distinguishing between; δ. φωνῆς καὶ σιγῆς*, Arist. *Cael.* 2. 9. 1; *diagnosis*, Hipp. 901.

διαδέκτωρ, *one who receives from another*, an *inheritor*, Maneth. 4. 223.

διάδημα, a *binding together* or *around, band, fillet*, Xen. *Cyr.* 8. 3. 13.

διάδικος, *one party in a lawsuit*, Jo. Chrys.; cf. διαδικέω, to *contend at law*, and οἱ διαδικοῦντες, the *contending parties*, Plut. 2. 196 B; διαδικασμός, a *lawsuit*.

διάδοκις, a *cross-beam*, Hesych.

διάδοσις, a *giving from one to another, largess*, Dem. 44. 37.

διαδοχή, a *taking from another*, of a trierarch; δ. νεώς, Dem. 50. 1; *succession*, ἄλλος παρ᾽ ἄλλου, Aesch. *Agam.* 313; *relay*, Xen. *Cyr.* 1. 4. 17.

διάζωμα, a *girdle*, Thuc. 1. 6; an *isthmus*, Plut. *Phoc.* 13.

διάθεμα, a *placing together* in a certain order, *arrangement* of the stars in one's birth, Sext. *Emp.* 5. 53; cf. διατίθημι.

διάθεσις, a *putting together, placing one thing with reference to another*, and so a *placing in order, arrangement*, διάθεσις λέγεται τοῦ ἔχοντος μέρη τάξις, ἢ κατὰ τόπον ἢ κατὰ δύναμιν ἢ κατ᾽ εἶδος · θέσιν γὰρ δεῖ τινα εἶναι, ὥσπερ καὶ τοὔνομα δηλοῖ ἡ διάθεσις, Aristot. *Metaph.* 4. 19, p. 1022; δ. τῆς πολιτείας, Plat. *Laws* 922 B; τῶν ξενίων, Tim. 27 A; *transmitting* of property *by will*, testament=διαθήκη, Plat. *Laws* 922 B; πῶς δ᾽ ἂν τῆς διαθέσεως τοῦ τετελευτηκότος ἀμελήσαιμεν, ἣν ἐκεῖνος διέθετο οὐ παρανοῶν οὐδὲ γυναικὶ πεισθείς; Lys., πρὸς Τιμωνίδην; *transferring* by sale, Isoc. 224 B, Plut. *Sol.* 24; cf. διατίθημι; cf. also διαθιγή=τάξις, Aristot. *Metaph.* 1. 48; 7. 2. 2.

διαθέτης, an *arranger, collector*, Damasc. ap. Suid., Hdt. 7. 6; cf. διατίθημι.

διαίρεσις, *division; ἐν διαρέσει ψήφων*, in the *reckoning* of the votes *on either side*, Aesch. *Eum.* 749.

διάκονος, a *messenger*, Aesch. *Prom.* 942.

διάκρισις, *decision*, judgment, Plat. *Laws* 765 A; the *space between* the eyes, Xen. *Venat.* 4. 1.

διάλεκτος, *discourse, conversation,* Plat. *Symp.* 203 A; *debate, argument,* Plat. *Rep.* 454 A.

διάλογος, *dialogue,* Plat. *Soph.* 293 E; *id. Prot.* 335 D.

διαλλαγή, *exchange, commerce;* ὡς διαλλαγὰς ἔχοιμεν ἀλλήλοισιν ὧν πένοιτο γῆ, Eur. *Supp.* 209; *reconciliation, truce,* Hdt. 1. 22.

διάλλαγμα, *a substitute,* Eur. *Hel.* 586.

διάλυσις, a *loosing from another, divorce,* Plut. *Sull.* 35; *treaty,* Aristot. *Pol.* 4. 14. 3.

διάνδιχα, adv., *two ways;* διάνδιχα μεμηρίζειν, to *halt between two opinions, Il.* 1. 189.

δίαυλος, a *double pipe, channel,* or *course,* Pind. *O.* 13. 50; *ebb and flow,* Eur. *Hec.* 29; *a strait,* Eur. *Tro.* 435.

δίβαμος, *on two legs,* Eur. *Rhes.* 215.

διβολία, a *double-edged lance,* Aristoph. *Frag.* 401.

CHAPTER II

CHRONOLOGICAL CONCORDANCE

427. ARISTOPHANES[1]

διαθήκη. *Vesp.* 584: κἂν ἀποθνήσκων ὁ πατήρ τῳ δῷ καταλείπων παῖδ᾽
ἐπίκληρον, κλάειν ἡμεῖς μακρὰ τὴν κεφαλὴν εἰπόντες τῇ δ.

διαθήκην. *Vesp.* 589: τῆς δ᾽ ἐπικλήρου τὴν δ. ἀδικεῖς ἀνακογχυλιάζων.

Av. 440: ἢν μὴ διάθωνταί γ᾽ οἵδε δ. ἐμοὶ ἥνπερ ὁ πίθηκος τῇ γυναικὶ διέθετο,

400. LYSIAS[2]

διαθήκην. 32. 5: δ. αὐτῷ δίδωσι καὶ πέντε τάλαντα ἀργυρίου παρακαταθήκην.

διαθῆκαι. 19. 39: ὁ γὰρ Κόνωνος θάνατος καὶ αἱ δ., ἃς διέθετο ἐν Κύπρῳ.

394. ISOCRATES[3]

διαθήκην. 19. 3: τεθνεῶτος αὐτοῦ πειρᾶται τήν τε δ. ἄκυρον . . . .
ποιῆσαι.

5: ὁ πατὴρ τοῦ καταλιπόντος τὴν δ.

15: ὁ τὴν δ. καταλιπών,

47: τὸν τὴν δ. καταλιπόντα.

διαθήκαις. 19. 1: ταῖς δ. αἷς ἐκεῖνος κατέλιπεν.

διαθήκας. 19. 12: υἱόν μ᾽ ἐποιήσατο . . . . τὴν οὐσίαν ἔδωκεν. καί μοι λαβὲ τὰς δ.

Ibid.: κατὰ γὰρ τοῦτον (τὸν νόμον) ἔδει ποιεῖσθαι τὰς δ.

15: τὰς μὲν δ. αὐτοὶ προσομολογοῦσι Θρασύλοχον καταλιπεῖν,

Ibid.: ζητοῦσι πείθειν ὑμᾶς, ὡς χρὴ τὰς δ. ἀκύρους ποιῆσαι.

34: τὰς μὲν δ. οὐκ ἀπιστοῦσι, Θρασύλοχον καταλιπεῖν,

44: εἰ τὰς τῶν παίδων δ. ἀκύρους ἴδοι γενομένας.

50: δ. παρ᾽ αὐτῶν τῶν ἀντιδίκων ὁμολογουμένας,

390. ISAEUS[3]

διαθήκη. 6. 7: καὶ ὑμῖν ἥ τε δ. αὕτη ἀναγνωσθήσεται καὶ οἱ παραγινόμενοι
μαρτυρήσουσι.

32: ὡς οὐκέτ᾽ αὐτῷ κέοιτο ἡ δ.

διαθήκη. 2. 44: οὐ λόγῳ οὐδὲ δ. τὴν ποίησιν γεγενημένην, ἀλλ᾽ ἔργῳ·

3. 56: τοῖς μεμαρτυρηκόσιν ἐπὶ τῇ δ. τοῦ Πύρρου παραγενέσθαι.

6. 7: καὶ ἔγραψεν οὕτως ἐν δ., εἰ μὴ γένοιτο αὐτῷ παιδίον ἐκ τῆς γυναικός,
τοῦτον κληρονομεῖν τῶν ἑαυτοῦ.

28: τοῖς γὰρ φύσει αὐτοῦ υἱέσιν οὐδεὶς οὐδενὶ ἐν δ. γράφει δόσιν οὐδεμίαν,

[1] Dunbar, *Concordance*, 1883. [2] Holmes, *Index*, 1895. [3] Personally examined.

διαθήκην. 1. 19: μᾶλλον βεβαιοῦν τὴν δ. βουλόμενον, ἣν ὀργιζόμενος
ἐποιήσατο.

41: τοῖς κατὰ γένος ψηφίζεσθαι μᾶλλον ἢ τοῖς κατὰ δ. ἀμφισβητοῦσι.

5. 6: ἀποθανόντος δ' αὐτοῦ ἄπαιδος δ. ἀπέφηνε Πρόξενος ὁ Δικαιογένους
πατήρ, ᾗ πιστεύσαντες οἱ ἡμέτεροι πατέρες ἐνείμαντο τὸν κλῆρον.

6. 4: καὶ τὴν δ. ἄκυρον ποιήσειν.

7: καὶ τὴν δ. κατέθετο παρὰ τῷ κηδεστῇ Χαιρέᾳ,

27: καὶ γράψας δ., ἐφ' οἷς εἰσήγαγε τὸν παῖδα κατατίθεται μετὰ τούτων
παρὰ Πυθοδώρῳ Κηφισιεῖ, προσήκοντι αὐτῷ.

30: πείθουσι τὸν Εὐκτήμονα τὴν μὲν δ. ἀνελεῖν

31: ἔλεγεν ὅτι βούλοιτ' ἀνελέσθαι τὴν δ.

8. 40: οὐδεμίαν ἐκείνου περὶ τούτων ποιησαμένου δ.

10. 10: παιδὸς γὰρ οὐκ ἔξεστι δ. γενέσθαι·

Ibid.: ὥστε κατά γε δ. ἐκείνων, οὐδ' εἰ διέθεντο προσῆκεν αὐτῷ τούτων τῶν
χρημάτων κληρονομῆσαι

11. 9: λαμβάνει δὲ τὸν κλῆρον Γλαύκων κατὰ τὴν δ.

Ibid.: νικήσασα τοὺς κατὰ τὴν δ. ἀμφισβητήσαντας.

18: τὸ προνενικηκέναι τοὺς κατὰ δ. ἀμφισβητήσαντας,

Fr. 1. 1: μετὰ ταύτην τοίνυν τὴν ἀπόκρισιν ἑτέραν δ. ἐκόμισαν, ἣν ἔφασαν
Ἀρχέπολιν ἐν Λήμνῳ διάθεσθαι.

διαθήκαιν. 5. 15: ταύταιν δὲ ταῖν δ. ἣν μὲν Πρόξενος ἀπέφηνε, Δικαιογένης
ἔπεισε τοὺς δικαστὰς ὡς οὐκ ἀληθὴς εἴη·

16: ἀμφοῖν δὲ ταῖν δ. ἀκύροιν γιγνομέναιν,

διαθῆκαι. 5. 15: δύω γὰρ δ. ἀπεφάνησαν, ἡ μὲν πάλαι πολλῷ, ἡ δ' ὕστερον·

9. 27: ὡς μὲν οὖν οὐκ εἰσὶν ἀληθεῖς αἱ δ.

διαθηκῶν. 1. 13: καίτοι χρὴ θεωρεῖν αὐτοῦ τὴν διάνοιαν ἐκ τούτων τῶν ἔργων
μᾶλλον ἢ ἐκ τῶν δ.

34: εἰ κατηγορεῖν ἐβούλοντο τῶν δ. ἢ τοῦ τελευτηκότος,

4. 6: οὐ μόνον περὶ τῶν δ. ἀλλὰ καὶ περὶ τοῦ γένους λόγον ἐμβεβλήκασιν.

12: περὶ μὲν γὰρ τῶν ἄλλων συμβαλαίων οὐ πάνυ χαλεπὸν τοὺς τὰ
ψευδῆ μαρτυροῦντας ἐλέγχειν. ζῶντας γὰρ καὶ παρόντος τοῦ πράξαντος
καταμαρτυροῦσι· περὶ δὲ τῶν δ. πῶς ἄν τις γνοίη τοὺς μὴ τἀληθῆ
λέγοντας,

9. 10: περί γε δ. οὔσης τῆς ἀμφισβητήσεως

14: σκέψασθε δέ, ὦ ἄνδρες, καὶ ἐκ τοῦ χρόνου ὃν οὗτοι λέγουσι περὶ τῶν δ.

Fr. 1. 2: δ. δὲ τεττάρων ὑπ' αὐτῶν ἐσκευοποιημένων.

διαθήκαις. 1. 3: οὗτοι μὲν δ. ἰσχυριζόμενοι τοιαύταις, ἃς ἐκεῖνος διέθετο.

18: ἰσχυρίζονται γὰρ ταῖς δ. λέγοντες ὡς Κλεώνυμος μετεπέμπετο τὴν
ἀρχὴν οὐ λῦσαι βουλόμενος αὐτὰς ἀλλ' ἐπανορθῶσαι καὶ βεβαιῶσαι
σφίσιν αὐτοῖς τὴν δωρεάν.

διαθήκαις. 1. 24: ἐν ταῖς νῦν γεγραμμέναις δ. ἔδωκεν αὐτοῖς τὴν οὐσίαν,

  2. 14: ἐμὲ ποιεῖται, οὐκ ἐν δ., ὦ ἄνδρες, γράψας, μέλλων ἀποθνήσκειν,

  3. 60: ὅσοι δὲ δ. αὐτοῖς εἰσποιοῦνται, τοῖς υἱοῖς ἐπιδικάζεσθαι προσήκει τῶν δοθέντων.

  4. 13: τἀναντία ταῖς τοῦ τεθνεῶτος δ. μεταγραφῆναι·

 Ibid.: οὐδὲν γὰρ μᾶλλον οἱ μάρτυρες εἴσονται, εἰ ἐφ' αἷς ἐκλήθησαν δ., αὗται ἀποφαίνονται.

  17: χωρὶς δὲ τούτων ταῖς μὲν δ. διὰ μαρτύρων ὑμᾶς δεῖ πιστεῦσαι, ὑφ' ὧν ἔνι καὶ ἐξαπατηθῆναι,

  24: οὐ γὰρ εἰς τοῦτό γε ἀνοίας ἥκουσιν ὥστε πιστεύσαντες ταῖς διαθήκαις οὕτω ῥᾳδίως τοσούτων χρημάτων ἀφίστανται.

  7. 2: ὁ δ' ἐν δ. σημηνάμενος ἀδήλους ἐποίησέ, διὸ πολλοὶ πεπλάσθαι φάσκοντες αὐτὰς ἀμφισβητεῖν ἀξιοῦσι πρὸς τοὺς ποιηθέντας.

  9. 13: ἀλλὰ μὴν οὐδ' αἰσχυνθῆναι οὐδενὶ προσήκει ἐπὶ ταῖς δ. ὡς πλείστους μάρτυρας παρίστασθαι, νόμου γε ὄντος ἐξεῖναι ὅτῳ βούλοιτο δοῦναι τὰ ἑαυτοῦ.

  18: οἶδ' ὅτι οὐκ ἂν ἐθελήσειε μαρτυρῆσαι ἐναντία ταῖς δ. αἷς αὐτὸς ἀποφαίνει.

  11. 8: εἰ δέ τι καὶ αὐτὴ πάθοι, Γλαύκωνι τὰ ὄντα ἐδίδου, ἀδελφῷ ὄντι ὁμομητρίῳ· καὶ ταῦτ' ἐν δ. ἐνέγραψε.

διαθήκας. 1. 10: ἐκ ταύτης τῆς ὀργῆς Κλεώνυμος ταύτας ποιεῖται τὰς δ.,

  11: εἰτ' ὀρθῶς εἴτε μή, τὰς δ. ταύτας διέθετο. .

  14: ἐβουλήθη ταύτας τὰς δ. ἀνελεῖν καὶ προσέταξε Ποσειδίππῳ τὴν ἀρχὴν εἰσαγαγεῖν.

  15: οὐχ ἡμῖν ἐγκαλῶν ἀλλὰ Δεινίᾳ πολεμῶν ταύτας τὰς δ. διέθετο,

  18: ὑμεῖς δὲ σκοπεῖσθε τὰς δ. τὰς μετ' ὀργῆς γενομένας πότερα εἰκός ἐστι βουληθῆναι Κλεώνυμον ἀνελεῖν, ἐπειδὴ πρὸς ἡμᾶς οἰκείως ἔσχεν, ἢ σκοπεῖν ὅπως ἔτι βεβαιότερον ἡμᾶς ἀποστερήσει τῶν αὐτοῦ.

  20: ἡμᾶς κακῶς ποιεῖν τε καὶ διατίθεσθαι τοιαύτας δ.

  21: εἰ μὲν γὰρ ἀνελεῖν τὰς δ. βουλόμενος μετεπέμπετο τὴν ἀρχήν,

 Ibid.: δικαίως ἂν δήπου τὰς τοιαύτας δ. ἀκύρους ποιήσαιτε.

  26: εἰ τοίνυν καὶ τοῦτο συγχωρήσαιμεν, ὡς ἐκεῖνος ἐπανορθῶσαι τὰς δ. ἐβούλετο,

 Ibid.: οἵ τινες ταύτας τὰς δ. ἀξιοῦσιν εἶναι κυρίας,

  30: ὥσπερ ὅτε τὰς δ. ταύτας ἐποιήσατο,

  34: οἵ γε τὰς δ. μὲν ἀποφαίνουσιν οὔτ' ὀρθῶς ἐχούσας οὔτ' ἀρεσκούσας τῷ διαθεμένῳ,

  35: τίς ἂν ὑμῶν ταύτας εἶναι κυρίας τὰς δ. ψηφίσαιτο ἃς ὁ μὲν διαθέμενος ὡς οὐκ ὀρθῶς ἐχούσας ἀπεδοκίμασεν, οὗτοι δ' ἔργῳ λύουσιν ἐθέλοντες ἡμῖν ἰσομοιρῆσαι τῆς οὐσίας.

διαθήκας. 1. 41: δ. δ᾽ ἤδη πολλοί ψευδεῖς ἀπέφηναν, καὶ οἱ μὲν τὸ παράπαν
οὐ γενομένας, ἐνίων δ᾽ οὐκ ὀρθῶς βεβουλευμένων.

42: τὰς δὲ δ., αἷς οὗτοι πιστεύοντες ἡμᾶς συκοφαντοῦσιν,

Ibid.: τὰς δὲ δ. ὑφ᾽ ἡμῶν ἀμφισβητουμένας· οὗτοι γὰρ τὸ ἀνελεῖν αὐτὰς
ἐκείνου βουλομένου διακώλυσαν.

43: πολὺ κάλλιόν ἐστι ψηφίσασθαι κατὰ τὸ γένος τὸ παρ᾽ ἀμφοτέρων
ἡμῶν ὁμολογούμενον μᾶλλον ἢ κατὰ τὰς δ. τὰς οὐ δικαίως γεγενη-
μένας.

48: διέθετο ταύτας τὰς δ. καὶ οὐδὲ πώποτε ὕστερον αὐτῷ μετεμέλησε,

50: ἐκεῖνόν τε νομίζειν ὀρθῶς βεβουλεῦσθαι λῦσαι τὰς δ. βουλόμενον,

4. 13: τῶν διατιθεμένων οἱ πολλοὶ οὐδὲ λέγουσι τοῖς παραγιγνομένοις ὅ τι
διατίθενται, ἀλλ᾽ αὐτοῦ μόνου, τοῦ καταλιπεῖν δ.

14: ὁ νόμος, ὦ ἄνδρες, οὐκ ἐάν τις διαθῆται μόνον, κυρίας εἶναι τὰς δ.,
ἀλλὰ ἐὰν εὖ φρονῶν.

Ibid.: σκεπτέον δὴ ὑμῖν πρῶτον μὲν εἰ ἐποιήσατο τὰς δ., ἔπειτα εἰ μὴ
παρανοῶν διέθετο.

15: ἀντιλεγόντων δ᾽ ἡμῶν μηδὲ τὸ παράπαν γενέσθαι τὰς δ.,

18: οἱ κατὰ τὰς δ. ἀμφισβητοῦντες.

Ibid.: μᾶλλον εἰκὸς ἦν ἀληθεῖς εἶναι δόξειν τὰς δ.

22: τὰς δ. σκοπεῖν, εἰ δοκοῦσι γενέσθαι·

9. 1: οὔτε ἐποιήσατο ἐκεῖνος υἱὸν ἑαυτῷ, οὔτ᾽ ἔδωκε τὰ ἑαυτοῦ, οὔτε δ.
κατέλιπεν,

2: δ. ψευδεῖς κατεσκεύασαν καὶ ζητοῦσιν ἀποστερῆσαι με τῶν τοῦ
ἀδελφοῦ.

5: καὶ τούτων δ. καταλίποι παρὰ Ἱεροκλεῖ Ἡφαιστιάδῃ,

6: ἀπεκρίνατό μοι ὅτι ἔχοι τὰς δ.

7: ἐλέγχειν ψευδεῖς οὔσας τὰς δ. ἃς ἐποιήσαντο.

8: εἰ μὴ ἄνευ τῶν οἰκείων τῶν ἑαυτοῦ τὰς δ. ποιοῖτο,

11: ὅτε τὸν υἱὸν τὸν τούτου ἐποιεῖτο Ἀστύφιλος καὶ τὰς δ. κατέλειπε,

12: εἰ μὲν ὁ Ἀστύφιλος μηδένα ἐβούλετο εἰδέναι ὅτι τὸν Κλέωνος υἱὸν
ἐποιεῖτο μηδ᾽ ὅτι δ. καταλίποι,

Ibid.: εἰ δ᾽ ἐναντίον μαρτύρων φαίνεται διαθέμενος, τούτων δὲ μὴ τῶν μάλιστα χρωμένων ἀλλὰ τῶν ἐντυχόντων, πῶς εἰκός ἐστιν ἀληθεῖς εἶναι
τὰς δ.;

14: καὶ οὐδ᾽ ἐν μιᾷ τούτων τῶν ἐξόδων δ. κατέλιπεν.

15: πῶς τοῦτον πιστὸν ἤδη τὰς δ. τότε καταλιπεῖν καὶ ἐκπλεύσαντα
τελευτῆσαι;

22: ἀλλ᾽ Ἱεροκλῆς, θεῖος ὢν καὶ ἐκείνῳ καὶ ἐμοί, οὕτως ἐστὶ τολμηρὸς
ὥστε οὐ γενομένας δ. ἥκει φέρων, καί φησι παρ᾽ ἑαυτῷ Ἀστύφιλον
ταύτας καταλιπεῖν.

διαθήκας. 9. 24: λέγων ὅτι θεῖος εἴη Ἀστυφίλῳ καὶ ἀποφανοίη δ. ἐκεῖνον
καταλελοιπότα,

    25: ὡς δὲ ἐπηγγέλλετο περιὼν δ. ἀποφανεῖν,

    26: οὐδὲ Κλέωνι προῖκα τὰς δ. ἀποφαίνει,

    31: εἰ καὶ δεκάκις ὁ Ἱεροκλῆς δ. ψευδεῖς ἀποδεικνύει,

    32: ἔπειτα νῦν ἀξιώσουσι κληρονομεῖν τῶν Ἀστυφίλου οὐ μόνον τὰς δ.
λέγοντες, ἀλλὰ καὶ τὸ γένος προστιθέντες,

  10. 9: κατὰ δ. αἱ εἰσαγωγαὶ τῶν εἰσποιήτων γίγνονται,

    10: οὐδετέρω αὐτῶν ἐξῆν δ. ποιήσασθαι.

    22: οὐ δίκαιόν ἐστι τὰς ἐκείνου δ. ἀκύρους καθιστάναι.

Ibid.: οἶμαι δεῖν κυρίας εἶναι τὰς δ. ἃς ἂν ἕκαστος διαθῆται περὶ τῶν ἑαυτου,

Ibid.: περὶ μέντοι τῶν ἀλλοτρίων οὐ κυρίας τὰς δ.

11. 9: ἡμεῖς δ' οὐ πώποτ' ἠξιώσαμεν ἀμφισβητῆσαι πρὸς τὰς ἐκείνου δ.

Ibid.: οὐδὲ πρὸς τὰς δ. ἠμφισβητήσαμεν.

387. PLATO[1]

διαθήκης. 923 Ε: φανῇ κλῆρος ἐπιχώριος τῆς δ. γενόμενος ὕοτερον,

  926 Β: ἐάν τινες ἄρα περὶ δ. ἐγκαλῶσι τοῖς κειμένοις νόμοις,

διαθήκην. 922 C: εἴ τις ἐξουσίαν δώσει ἁπλῶς οὕτω κυρίαν εἶναι δ., ἢ ἄν τις
διαθῆται ὁπωσοῦν ἔχων πρὸς τῷ τοῦ βίου τέλει.

  923 C: ὃς ἂν δ. γράφῃ τὰ αὑτοῦ διατιθέμενος, παίδων ὢν πατήρ, πρῶτον μὲν
τῶν υἱέων κληρονόμον ὃν ἂν ἀξιώσῃ γίγνεσθαι γραφέτω.

    Ε: τῷ κληρονόμῳ τοῦ τὴν δ. διαθεμένῳ καταλειπέτω.

Ibid.: γραφέτω καὶ περὶ τῆς τοιαύτης τύχης ὁ τὴν δ. γράφων.

  924 Α: ἐὰν δέ τις ἄπαις ὢν τὸ παράπαν δ. γράφῃ,

362. DEMOSTHENES[2]

διαθήκη. 45. 11: εἶθ' ἡ δ. γέγραπται.

Ibid.: τοῦ τις ἂν εἵνεκ' ἔφυγεν ἀνοίγειν τὸ γραμματεῖον. ἵν' ἡ δ. νὴ Δία μὴ
φανερὰ γένοιτο τοῖς δικασταῖς.

    18: γραμματεῖον ἔχειν ἐφ' ᾧ γεγράφθαι "δ. Πασίωνος,"

    21: εἰ δ' ὥσπερ μεμαρτύρηκεν, ἐπῆν "δ. Πασίωνος,"

    22: ἐξελέγχεται κατεσκευασμένη μὲν ἡ δ.,

    29: ὄψεσθ' ὅτι πλάσμ' ὅλον ἐστὶν ἡ δ.

  46. 25: ἄκυρος μὲν ἡ δ. ἐστίν, ἥν φασιν οὗτοι τὸν πατέρα καταλιπεῖν,

---

[1] Ast, *Index*, 1855; E. Abbott, *Subject Index*, 1875.

[2] Preuss, *Index*, 1892.

διαθήκης. 29. 42: μάλιστα δ' εἰ περὶ τῆς δ. ἀκούσειεν.

    43: τὸ μισθοῦν τὸν οἶκον ἠφάνιζεν ἐκ τῆς δ.

  36. 7: λαβὲ τῆς δ. τὸ ἀντίγραφον

    32: οὐ μόνον ἐκ τῆς δ. ἔστιν ἰδεῖν

    34: οὐ γὰρ ἐκεῖνό γ' ἐρεῖ, ὡς ὅσα μὲν πλεονεκτεῖν τόνδ' ἔγραψ' ὁ πατήρ, κύρι' ἐστὶ τῆς δ., τὰ δ' ἀλλ' ἄκυρα.

  45. 5: μάρτυρας παρέσχετο ψευδεῖς δ. οὐδεπώποτε γενομένας.

    21: εἰ μὲν γὰρ ἐπῆν ἐπὶ τῆς δ. "Πασίωνος καὶ Φορμίωνος," ἢ "πρὸς Φορμίων'" ἢ τοιοῦτό τι,

    27: τὸ κατασεύασμα τὸ τῆς δ.

Ibid.: ὅτι δ' οὕτω ταῦτ' ἔχει, τῆς δ. αὐτῆς ἀκούσαντες γνώσεσθε·

    30: τῶν μὲν οἴκοι χρημάτων διὰ τῆς δ. αὐτὸν ἐποίησε κύριον,

    41: κατεσκευασμένης δ. μάρτυς γεγονώς.

  46. 18: κατεσκευασμένης δ. ψευδὴς μάρτυς γέγονε

    25: ἀντίγραφά ἐστι τῆς δ. τῆς Πασίωνος·

    28: ὅτι δ. οὐδεὶς πώποτε ἀντίγραφα ἐποιήσατο,

διαθήκῃ. 29. 29: τὸν οἶκον οὐκ ἐμίσθωσε τῶν νόμων κελευόντων καὶ τοῦ πατρὸς ἐν τῇ δ. γράφοντος,

    42: τὰ καταλειφθέντα πάντ' ἐν τῇ δ. γράψαντος,

    43: ἦν δὲ ταῦθ' ἃ γεγράφθαι φησὶν ἐν τῇ δ.

  36. 52: ἐναντία τῇ δ. καὶ ταῖς ἀπ' ἐκείνης ἀραῖς,

  45. 15: ἐκ τοῦ πρόκλησιν ὁμοῦ δ. μαρτυρεῖν.

    42: ἐναντία δ', ἣν ἀνέγνων ὑμῖν ἄρτι, μίσθωσις τῇδε τῇ δ.

διαθήκην. 27. 13: οὗτος γὰρ εὐθὺς μετὰ τὸν τοῦ πατρὸς θάνατον ᾤκει τὴν οἰκίαν εἰσελθὼν κατὰ τὴν ἐκείνου δ.

    42: οὗτος δ. μὲν γενέσθαι φησί,

    43: οὗτος αὖ τὴν μὲν δ. γενέσθαι φησί,

    48: πρὸς δὲ τούτοις τὴν δ. ἠφανικότα,

    64: οἳ καὶ τὴν δ. ἠφανίκασιν ὡς λήσοντες,

  28. 5: τὴν μὲν δ. μηδαμοῦ ταύτην ἀποφαίνειν,

    6: αὐτὴν δὲ τὴν δ. δι' ἧς καὶ τούτων ὧν ἐσημήναντο γραμμάτων . . . . ἐγίγνοντο κύριοι, καὶ τοῦ μὴ μισθοῦν τὸν οἶκον τῆς αἰτίας ἀπελέλυντο, ταύτην δ' οὐκ ἐσημήναντο, οὐδ' αὐτὴν ἀπέδοσαν.

    10: τὴν μὲν δ. ἠφανίκατε, ἐξ ἧς ἦν εἰδέναι περὶ πάντων τὴν ἀλήθειαν,

  29. 31: ἣν ἔλαβε προῖκα τῆς μητρὸς κατὰ τὴν δ. τοῦ πατρός.

    33: λαβεῖν τὴν προῖκα τοῦτον τὴν ἑαυτῆς κατὰ τὴν τοῦ πατρὸς δ.

    57: τὴν δ. οὐκ ἀποδόντα,

  36. 8: τὴν μὲν γυναῖκα λαμβάνει κατὰ τὴν δ.

    33: ἐτόλμα λέγειν . . . . ἕνα μὲν τὸ παράπαν μὴ γενέσθαι δ., ἀλλ' εἶναι τοῦτο πλάσμα καὶ σκευώρημ' ὅλον,

διαθήκην.   36. 34: ὅταν μὲν τοίνυν τὴν δ. ἀρνῆται, ἐκ τίνος τρόπου πρεσβεῖα

Ibid.:   λαβὼν τὴν συνοικίαν κατὰ τὴν δ. ἔχει, τοῦτ' ἐρωτᾶτ' αὐτόν.

     35: πρεσβεῖά τε τὴν συνοικίαν ἔλαβεν κατὰ τὴν δ.

     45. 9: τοῦτό γ' αὐτὸ θαυμάζειν, τὸ τὴν μὲν ἀρχὴν τῆς μαρτυρίας εἶναι
πρόκλησιν, τὴν δὲ τελευτὴν δ.

     12: εἰ μὲν τοίνυν μὴ προσεμαρτύρουν τῇ προκλήσει τὴν δ. οὗτοι,

Ibid.:   παρεῖχέν τις αὐτοῖς γραμματεῖον ὡς δ.

     19: οἱ μὲν δικασταὶ ταύτην τὴν δ. ἐπίστευσαν τοῦ πατρὸς εἶναι,

     28: λέγε δ' αὐτοῖς τὴν δ. αὐτήν, ἣν οὗτοι μετὰ τῆς προκλήσεως μεμαρτυ-
ρήκασιν·

     34: τοῦ τὴν δ. ψευδῆ δεῖξαι,

Ibid.:   τοῦτο τοίνυν τὸ γράμμα παντελῶς δηλοῖ ψευδῆ τὴν δ οὖσαν.

     37: ἐμαρτύρησε μέν Νικοκλῆς ἐπιτροπεῦσαι κατὰ τὴν δ.,

Ibid.:   ἐμαρτύρησε δὲ Πασικλῆς ἐπιτροπευθῆναι κατὰ τὴν δ.

     38: ἐπιτροπεῦσαι μὲν κατὰ δ. οὐδὲν δεινὸν ἡγεῖτο μαρτυρεῖν ὁ μαρτυρῶν,

Ibid.:   οὐδ' ἐπιτροπευθῆναι κατὰ δ. ,

     39: οὐδὲ καταλιπεῖν τὸν πατέρ' αὐτῷ ἐπιγεγραμμένον γραμματεῖον δ.

     51: τοὺς δ. μαρτυρήσαντες θιῶκων,

Ibid.:   διὰ τοὺς ἀφεῖναι μεμαρτυρηκότας ἀποψηφίσασθαι μᾶλλον ἢ διὰ τοὺς
δ. μαρτυρήσαντας.

     46. 2: ὡς ἢ διατιθεμένῳ τῷ πατρὶ τῷ ἐμοῦ παρεγένετό που αὐτὸς ταύτην
τὴν δ.

     12: οὔτε διέθετο ὁ πατὴρ ἡμῶν δ. οὐδεμίαν, οὔθ' οἱ νόμοι ἐῶσιν.

     15: ὁ τοίνυν πατὴρ ἡμῶν ἐπεποίητο ὑπὸ τοῦ δήμου πολίτης, ὥστε οὐδὲ
κατὰ τοῦτο ἐξῆν αὐτῷ διαθέσθαι δ.

     24: σκέψασθε δὴ καὶ τονδὶ τὸν νόμον, ὃς κελεύει τὴν δ. , ἣν ἂν παίδων
ὄντων γνησίων ὁ πατὴρ διαθῆται, ἐὰν ἀποθάνωσιν οἱ παῖδες πρὶν
ἡβῆσαι, κυρίαν εἶναι.

διαθῆκαι.   36. 7: τὰς μαρτυρίας ταυτασί, παρ' οἷς αἱ δ. κεῖνται.

     43. 4: αἱ δὲ δ. , ἃς τότε παρέσχοντο, ἐξηλέγχθησαν ψευδεῖς οὖσαι.

     45. 26: τί δ' ἡμεῖς ἴσμεν, εἴ τινές εἰσιν δ. Πασίωνος;

     46. 16: εἰ δοκοῦσιν ὑμῖν εὖ φρονοῦντος ἀνδρὸς εἶναι αἱ δ.,

διαθηκῶν.   27. 44: δῆλον τοίνυν ἐστὶν οὐδὲν ἧττον τὸ πλῆθος τῶν καταλει-
φθέντων, καίπερ ἀφανιζόντων τούτων τὴν οὐσίαν ἐκ τῶν δ. , ἐξ ὧν
τοσαῦτα χρήματ' ἀλλήλοις φασὶ δοθῆναι.

     45. 25: εἰ μή φησιν ἀντίγραφα εἶναι τῶν δ. τῶν Πασίωνος —

     26: "εἰ μή φημ' ἐγὼ ἀντίγραφα εἶναι τῶν δ.," οὕτως "ὧν φησι Φορμίων
Πασίωνα καταλιπεῖν," οὐ "τῶν Πασίωνος."

     46. 3: μεμαρτύρηκεν ἀντίγραφ' εἶναι τῶν δ. τῶν Πασίωνος τὰ ἐν τῷ γραμ-
ματείῳ γεγραμμένα,

διαθηκῶν. 46. 5: ἀντίγραφα δὲ τῶν δ. τῶν Πασίωνος μαρτυρεῖν εἶναι τὰ ἐν γραμματείῳ ὁ παρείλετο Φορμίων,

    28: ἄξιον τοίνυν ὦ ἄνδρες δικασταὶ καὶ τόδε ἐνθυμηθῆναι, ὅτι διαθήκης οὐδεὶς πώποτε ἀντίγραφα ἐποιήσατο, ἀλλὰ συγγραφῶν μέν, ἵνα εἰδῶσι καὶ μὴ παραβαίνωσι, δ. δὲ οὔ.

Ibid.: πῶς οὖν ὑμεῖς ἴστε ὅτι ἀντίγραφά ἐστι τῶν δ. τῶν Πασίωνος τὰ ἐν τῷ γραμματείῳ γεγραμμένα;

διαθήκαις. 28. 3: τέτταρα τάλαντα καὶ τρισχιλίας .... γραφῆναί τ' ἐν ταῖς δ.

    14: ταυθ' οὗτοι γεγραφῆναί τ' ἐν ταῖς δ. .... κατ' ἀλλήλων μαρτυροῦσι.

41. 16: τοὺς τὸ τελευταῖον ταῖς δ. παραγενομένους ·

45. 22: οὔτε ἐμαρτύρησεν ἐκεῖνος περὶ τῶν ἐν ταῖς δ. ἐνόντων οὐδέν.

    39: ἀφαιρῶν ἑκάτερος τὸ μαρτυρεῖν τὰ ἐν ταῖς δ. ὑπὸ τούτου γεγραμμένα,

διαθήκας. 27. 40: ἔτι δ' ἀκριβέστερον ἔγνωτ' ἄν, εἴ μοι τὰς δ. ἃς ὁ πατὴρ κατέλιπεν, οὗτοι ἀποδοῦναι ἠθέλησαν.

    28. 5: ἐχρῆν, ἐπειδὴ τάχιστ' ἐτελεύτησεν ὁ πατήρ, εἰσκαλέσαντας μάρτυρας πολλοὺς παρασμήνασθαι κελεῦσαι τὰς δ.

    36. 8: εἰ δεήσει κατὰ τὰς δ.

41. 17: ὅτε γὰρ Πολύευκτος διέθετο ταῦτα, παρῆν μὲν ἡ τούτου γυνή, καὶ δῆλον ὅτι τὰς τοῦ πατρὸς δ. ἀνήγγειλεν,

    43. 4: δ. δὲ ψευδεῖς ἧκον κατασκευάσαντες Γλαῦκός τε

    5: εἴ τις ἀμφισβητεῖν ἢ παρακαταβάλλειν βούλεται τοῦ κλήρου. τοῦ Ἁγνίου ἢ κατὰ γένος ἢ κατὰ δ.

44. 65: εἰ μὲν ὁ τελευτηκὼς ἐποιήσατό τινα .... συνεχωροῦμεν ἂν αὐτῷ, ἢ εἰ δ. κατελελοίπει, καὶ ταύταις ἂν ἐνεμείναμεν,

45. 10: προκαλεῖσθαι Φορμίων' ἀνοίγειν τὰς δ.

Ibid.: εἶναι δ' ἃς αὐτοὶ μεμαρτυρήκασιν δ. ἀντιγράφους ἐκείνων.

    11: οὐδέν πω λέγω, οὐδ' ὑπὲρ τοῦ τὰς δ. ἀληθεῖς ἢ ψευδεῖς εἶναι,

    19: οἶδε δὲ τῇ προκλήσει χρησάμενοι παραπετάσματι, δ. ἐμαρτύρησαν,

    26: τοῦτο μὲν γὰρ ἦν εἶναι δ. μαρτυρεῖν, ὅπερ ἦν τούτοις βούλημα,

    37: ὁ γὰρ ἐπιτροπεῦσαι κατὰ δ. μαρτυρῶν, δῆλον ὅτι καθ' ὁποῖος ἂν εἰδείη.

Ibid.: καὶ ὁ ἐπιτροπευθῆναι κατὰ δ. μαρτυρῶν, δῆλον ὅτι καθ' ὁποίας ἂν εἰδείη.

    38: τί οὖν μαθόντες ἐμαρτυρεῖθ' ὑμεῖς ἐν προκλήσει δ. ,

    39: δ. δὲ μαρτυρεῖν, ἐν αἷς χρημάτων τοσούτων κλοπή, ... οὐδεὶς ἤθελεν.

    41: τὰς δὲ συνθήκας καὶ τὰς δ. καὶ τἄλλ', ... σεσημασέν' ἐᾶσαι

διαθήκας. 45. 74: τί γὰρ αὐτὸν οἴεσθ' εἰς <u>τὰς δ.</u> ἐγράψαι, "καὶ τᾶλλα, ὅσα ἐστίν, Ἀρχίππῃ δίδωμι;"

     88: ἐὰν μεμαρτυρηκέναι τὸν μὲν ἐπιτροπευθῆναι κατὰ δ.

     46. 3: τὰς δὲ δ. μὴ ἔχει ἐπιδεῖξαι μήθ' ὡς ὁ πατὴρ διέθεθ' ἡμῶν,

     8: <u>οὖτ'</u> εἰδῶς δ. καταλιπόντα τὸν πατέρα ἡμῶν,

     13: ἀποθανόντα <u>δ.</u> καταλιπεῖν, ᾶς οὐ κύριος ἦν;

     15: τοῦ μὲν νόμου ἀκηκόατε, ὃς οὐκ ἐᾷ δ. διαθέσθαι, ἐὰν παῖδες ὦσι γνήσιοι.

     19: ἢ μάρτυρας ψευδεῖς οἴεσθ' ἂν παρασχέσθαι καὶ δ. οὐκ οὔσας,

344. ARISTOTLE [1]

διαθῆκαι. *Prob.* 950. 3: δ. δὲ πολλαὶ ψευδεῖς ἤδη ἐξηλέγχθησαν οὖσαι.

διαθήκαις. *Ibid.:* διὰ τὶ ἐνίοις δικαστηρίοις τοῖς γένεσι μᾶλλον ἢ ταῖς δ. ψηφιοῦνται;

διαθήκας. Sent. Fr. 16; Didot IV, p. 339: ὁ ἐν νόσῳ δ. γράφων, παραπλήσια πάσχει τοῖς χειμῶνι θαλαττίῳ εὐτρεπίζειν ἀρχομένοις τὰ τῆς νηὸς ὅπλα.

324. DINARCHUS [2]

διαθήκας. I. 9: τὸ μὲν γὰρ συνέδριον . . . . ὁ φυλάττει <u>τὰς</u> ἀπορρήτους <u>δ.</u> , ἐν αἷς τὰ τῆς πόλεως σωτήρια κεῖται.

323. HYPEREIDES [3]

διαθῆκαι. v. 17: ὅπου δὲ οὐδε [περὶ] τῶν αὐτοῦ ἰδίων αἱ [ἐγγύα]ί καὶ αἱ δ. κύριαί εἰσιν,[4]

διαθηκῶν. *Ibid.:* ὁ περὶ τῶ[ν] δ. ν[όμο]ς παρ[α]πλήσιος τούτοις ἐστίν· κελεύε[ι γὰρ ἐξεῖν]αι τὰ ἑαυτοῦ [δια]τίθεσθα[ι ὡς ἄν] τις βούληται,

διαθήκαις. ii. 47. 26: πῶς οὐκ ἄτοπον, εἰ μέν τι ἔπαθεν τὸ παιδίον ἢ γιγνόμενον ἢ καὶ ὕστερον, ταύταις <u>ταῖς δ.</u> ἰσχυρίζεσθαι ἂν αὐτούς, ἐν αἷς . . . .

διαθήκας. v. 18: ἐὰν μέν τι[ς εἰ]ς δι[οίκ]ησιν τ[ῶ]ν αὐτοῦ [γυ]ναικὶ πειθόμενος διαθήκα[ς γρά]ψῃ, ἄκυροι ἔσο[νται]·

---

[1] Bonitz, *Index* in *Acad. Reg. Bor.*, 1870.

[2] Forman, *Index*, 1896.

[3] Blass, *Index*, 1894.

[4] αἱ ἐ[γγύα]ι καὶ αἱ, Revillout, *editio princeps* (in *Corpus Papyrorum Aegypti*). αἱ [μὴ δ]ίκαιαι, Blass, Teubner ed., 1894.

APPENDIX TO CHAPTER II

It is thought advisable, for the sake of completeness, to append to this concordance a chronological catalogue of authors in whose writings the term does not occur. I have made a personal examination in all cases where an index is not named in a footnote. The number preceding each name is the "floruit."

900 B. C. ?, Homer;[1] 800 ?, Hesiod;[2] 800 ?, Homeric Hymns;[1] 730, Callinus Ephesius, Eleg.; 700, Archilochus Parius, Iambog.; 700, Asius, Eleg.; 693, Simonides Amorginus, Lyr.; 650, Alcman, Lyr.; 650, Tyrtaeus, Eleg.; 647, Pisander Rhodius, Lyr.; 630, Mimnermus, Eleg.; 611, Sappho, Lyr.; 611, Stesichorus, Lyr.; 610, Erinna, Lyr.; 606, Alcaeus Myrtilenaeus, Lyr.; 594, Solon, Eleg.; 580, Anaximander Phil.; 575, Acusilaus, Histor.; 570, Susario, Com.; 560, Ibycus, Lyr.; 546, Hipponax, Iambog.; 544, Anaximenes, Phil.; 544, Pherecydes (of Syros), Phil.; 544, Theognis, Eleg.; 540, Anacreon, Lyr.; 540, Ananias, Iambog.; 540, Phocylides, Eleg.; 538, Xenophanes, Phil.; 531, Pythagoras, Phil.; 525, Simonides Ceïus, Lyr.; 523, Choerilus Atticus, Trag.;[3] 520, Hecataeus Milesius, Hist.; 513, Heraclitus, Phil.; 510, Telesilla, Lyr.; 508, Lasus, Dithyr.; 504, Charon, Hist.; 503, Parmenides, Phil.; 500, Corinna, Lyr.; 500, Lamprocles, Dithyr.; 500, Timocreon, Phil.; 499, Pratinas, Lyr.; 490, Pindar, Lyr.;[4] 489, Panyasis, Epic; 487, Dinolochus, Com.; 487, Chionides, Com.; 484, Aeschylus, Trag.;[5] 480, Pherecydes, Hist.; 477, Epicharmus, Com.; 475, Phrynichus, Trag.; 470, Bacchylides, Lyr.; 470, Diocles, Com.;[6] 468, Sophocles, Trag.:[7] 466, Hellanicus, Hist.; 464, Zeno Eleaticus; 463, Xanthus, Phil.; 460, Ecphantides, Com.;[6] 460, Magnes, Com.; 454, Cratinus Major, Com.;[6] 451, Ion Chius, Trag.; 450, Anaxagoras, Phil.; 450 ?, Melanippides, Dithyr.; 450, Praxilla, Lyr.; 450, Aristias, Trag.; 450, Sophron, Mimog.;[8] 449, Crates, Com.;[6] 444, Melissus, Phil.; 444, Empedocles, Phil.; 444, Achaeus Eretrieus, Trag.;[3] 443, Herodotus, Hist.;[9] 441, Euripides, Trag.;[10] 440, Antiphon, Orat.;[11] 440, Teleclides, Com.;[6] 440, Choerilus Samius, Epic;[12] 438, Pherecrates, Com.; 434, Lysippus, Com.;[6] 432, Hermippus, Com.; 432, Amipsias, Com.; 432, Alcidamus, Rhet.; 430, Hippocrates, Med.; 430, Democritus, Phil.; 430, Philonides, Com.;[6] 430, Myrtilus, Com.; 429, Phrynicus, Com.; 429, Eupolis, Com.; 427, Plato, Com.; 427, Gorgias, Phil.; 425, Aristomenes, Com.; 424, Callias, Com.; 423, Amipsias, Com.; 423, Thucydides, Hist.;[13] 422, Leucon, Com,; 420, Cantharus, Com.; 420,

---

[1] Dunbar, *Concord.*, 1880.

[2] Paulson, *Index*, 1890; Capelle, *Lex.*, 1889.

[3] Nauck, *Index*, 1892.   [5] Wellauer, *Lex.*, 1830.   [7] Ellendt, *Index*, 1872.

[4] Rumpel, *Lex.*, 1883.   [6] Jacobi, *Index*, 1857.   [8] Kaibel, *Index*, 1899.

[9] Schweighaüser, *Lex.*, 1824; Sayce, *Index Eng.*, I–III, 1883; Macan, *Index Gr.*, 1895.

[10] Beck, *Index*, 1829.   [12] Näke, *Index*, 1817.

[11] Van Cleef, *Index*, 1895.   [13] Essen, *Index*, 1887.

Aristonymus, Com.; 416, Agathon, Trag.; 415, Andocides, Orat.;[1] 415, Archippus, Com.; 413, Hegemon, Com.; 411, Critias, Trag.;[2] 410, Aristagoras, Com.; 410, Metagenes, Com.; 407, Apollophanes, Com.; 407, Sannyrio, Com.; 407, Strattis, Com.; 405, Antimachus, Eleg.; 404, Philistus,[1] Hist.; 402, Polyzelus, Com.; 402, Cephisodorus, Com.; 401, Telestes, Lyr.; 401, Ctesias, Hist.; 401, Xenophon, Hist.;[3] 400 ?, Ocellus Lucanus, Phil.; 400, Euthycles, Com.; 400, Nicochares, Com.; 400 ?, Clitodemus, Hist.; 400 ?, Archytas, Phil.; 400, Demetrius, Com.; 400, Polyidus, Lyr.; 399, Cebes, Phil.;[4] 398, Astydamus, Trag.;[2] 398, Philoxenus, Lyr.; 398, Timotheus, Dithyr.; 394, Epilycus, Com.; 394, Eunicus, Com.; 392, Philyllius,Com.; 390, Theopompus, Com.; 390, Heraclides Ponticus, Pol.; 390, Autocrates, Com.; 388, Nicophon, Com ; 388, Alcaeus, Com.; 387, Antiphanes, Com.; 380, Ophelion, Com.; 380, Philiscus, Com.; 378, Epigenes, Com.; 376, Epicrates, Com.; 376, Anaximandres, Com.;[5] 375, Araros, Com.; 375, Eubulus, Com.;[5] 368, Ephippus, Com.; 366, Eudoxus, Astron.; 363, Diogenes, Cynic; 362, Aeneas Tacitus; 356, Alexis, Com.;[5] 354, Diodorus, Com.; 353, Chion, Hist.; 350, Aristophon, Com.; 350, Alexander, Com.; 350, Timotheus, Com; 350, Timocles, Com.; 350, Scylax, Geog.; 350, Philetaerus, Com.; 350, Nicostratus, Com.; 350, Ephorus, Hist.; 350, Calippus, Astron.; 350, Cratinus Minor, Com.; 350, Dionysius, Com.; 350, Dromon, Com.; 350 ?, Antidolus, Com.; 350 ?, Nausicrates, Com.; 350 ?, Heniochus, Com.; 350 ?, Eriphus, Com.; 350 ?, Callicrates, Com.; 350 ?, Athenion, Com.; 350 ?, Sophilus, Com.; 350 ?, Eubulides, Com.; 350, Amphis, Com.; 350, Xenarchus, Com.; 349, Demades, Orat.; 348, Heraclides, Com.; 347, Speusippus, Phil.; 345, Aeschines, Orat.;[6] 345, Damoxenus, Com.; 340, Anaxilas, Com.; 340, Anaximenes, Rhet.;[7] 340, Axionicus, Com.; 340, Hermesianax, Eleg.; 339, Xenocrates Chalcedonius; 333, Theopompus, Hist.; 332, Hecataeus Abderita, Hist.; 332, Stephanus, Com.; 330, Apollodorus, Com.; 330, Lycurgus, Orat.;[1] 330, Philemon, Com.;[5] 330, Theophilus, Com.; 327, Eudemus of Rhodes, Phil.; 324, Crobylus, Com.; 323, Philippides, Com.; 322, Theophrastus, Phil.; 322, Menander, Com.;[5] 322, Phanias, Phil.; 321, Philemon Minor, Com.; 320, Diphilus, Com.;[5] 320, Hipparchus, Com.; 320, Dicaearchus, Geog.; 317, Demetrius Phalerius, Rhet.; 306, Epicurus, Phil.; 303, Anaxippus, Com.; 302, Archedieus, Com.; 300, Euhemerus; 300, Hegesippus, Com.; 300 ?, Herondas; 300, Hieronymus Rhodius, Phil.; 300, Lynceus, Com.; 300, Philetas, Eleg.

[1] Forman, *Index*, 1897.   [2] Nauck, *Index*, 1892.

[3] Sturtz, *Lex.*, 1801; *Anab.*, Vollbrecht, *Lex.*, 1886; *Hell.*, Thiemann, *Lex.*, 1883; *Hist. Gr.*, Keller, *Index*, 1890; *Mem.*, Crusius, *Lex.*, 1844; *Oec.*, Holden, *Lex.*, 1895.

[4] Praechter, *Index*, 1893.   [6] Preuss, *Index*, 1896.

[5] Jacobi, *Index*, 1857.   [7] Bonitz, *Index*, 1870.

CHAPTER III

ΔΙΑΤΙΘΗΜΙ

The use of the verb διατίθημι has an important bearing on that of the noun διαθήκη, its derivative. The verb is often used to include the meaning of the noun; e. g., instead of διατίθεμαι διαθήκην we find simply διατίθεμαι. The verb has a much wider range of use, and is employed by authors in whose writings the noun is not found.

I. In the active it signifies, according to its derivation[1] to *put apart* or in two places, to *place separately*, and so it comes to mean —

1. To *place in order, distribute, arrange, dispose* (Lat. *dispono*): *Hymn to Ap.* 254, 294 of laying the foundation of a temple: διέθηκε θεμείλια Φοῖβος Ἀπόλλων εὐρέα καὶ μάλα μακρὰ διηνεκές.[2]

Herod. 7. 39, where Xerxes orders the son of a man who had offended him to be slain and his body to be divided in two, one half to be placed on the right side of the road and the other on the left, while the army marched between the parts: αὐτίκα ἐκέλευε τοῖσι προσετέτακτο ταῦτα πρήσσειν τῶν Πυθίου παίδων ἐξευρόντας τὸν πρεσβύτατον μέσον διαταμεῖν, διαταμόντας δὲ τὰ ἡμίτομα διαθεῖναι τὸ μὲν ἐπὶ δεξιὰ τῆς ὁδοῦ, τὸ δ' ἐπ' ἀριστερά, καὶ ταύτῃ διεξιέναι τὸν στρατόν.

Thuc. i. 126. 8, of *disposing* or *stationing* troops during a siege: χρόνου δὲ ἐπιγιγνομένου οἱ Ἀθηναῖοι τρυχόμενοι τῇ προσεδρείᾳ ἀπῆλθον οἱ πολλοί, ἐπιτρέψαντες τοῖς ἐννέα ἄρχουσι τὴν φυλακὴν καὶ τὸ πᾶν αὐτοκράτορσι διαθεῖναι ᾗ ἂν ἄριστα διαγιγνώσκωσι.

Xen. *Mem.* 2. 1. 27, in the parable of the choice of Hercules, of the gods *disposing* or *arranging* affairs so that blessings are the reward of virtue: οὐκ ἐξαπατήσω δέ σε προοιμίοις ἡδονῆς, ἀλλ' ᾗπερ οἱ θεοὶ διέθεσαν τὰ ὄντα διηγήσομαι μετ' ἀληθείας.

Arist. *A. M.* 8. 4, of *setting out* wine in earthen vessels to catch serpents: θηροῦσί τινες καὶ τοὺς ἔχεις εἰς ὀστράκια διαθέντες οἶνον εἰς τὰς αἱμασίας.

Timon in Diog. Laert. 8. 67, of a philosopher *setting forth* the first principles or elements; cf. Diels, *Poet. Phil. Fr.*, p. 194.

καὶ Ἐμπεδοκλῆς ἀγοραίων
ληπτὴς ἐπέων· ὅσα δ' ἔσθενε τοσσάδε εἶλεν
ἄρχων ὅς διέθηκ' ἀρχὰς ἐπδευέας ἄλλων.

---

[1] See chap. i.

[2] Allen and Sykes, *Homeric Hymns* (1904), say: "The verb [διατίθημι] is not found in Homer or Hesiod, and does not seem to occur elsewhere in serious poetry, though common in Attic prose." But see Eurip. *Ion.* 866. Its use is *rare* in poetry.

2. To *dispose* or *arrange* one's words in discourse, and so *to recite* (of rhapsodists, orators, and actors). Plato *Legg*. 658 D: ῥαψῳδὸν δέ, καλῶς Ἰλιάδα καὶ Ὀδύσσειαν ἤ τι τῶν Ἡσιοδείων διατιθέντα, ταχ᾿ ἂν ἡμεῖς οἱ γέροντες ἥδιστα ἀκούσαντες. *Id. Charm.* 162 D: ὀργισθῆναι αὐτῷ, ὥσπερ ποιήτης ὑποκριτῇ κακῶς διατιθέντι τὰ ἑαυτοῦ ποιήματα.

3. With an adverb, *to dispose* or *arrange* affairs well or ill, *to manage, handle, treat*.

a). *To manage*, of State affairs. *Lys.* 29. 2: κακῶς διαθεὶς τὰ τῆς πόλεως πλέον ἢ τριάκοντα ταλάντων οὐσίαν ἐκτήσατο. Of an estate, Isaeus 10. 25: οὐκ ἱκανόν ἐστι Ξεναινέτῳ τόν Ἀριστομένους οἶκον καταπεπαιδεραστη-κέναι, ἀλλὰ καὶ τοῦτον οἴεται δεῖν τὸν αὐτὸν τρόπον διαθεῖναι.

Of a campaign, Thuc. 6. 15: κράτιστα διαθέντι τὰ τοῦ πολέμου.

Of oneself or others, Archytas *Moral.* 1. 3: μὴ μόνον αὔταυτον οὕτω διατιθείς, etc.

b) *To handle*, or *treat* a person or thing in a certain manner. Of cities, Isoc. 4. (*Paneg.*) 113: τὰς ἑαυτῶν πόλεις οὕτως ἀνόμως διαθέντες καὶ τῆϡ ἡμετέρϡς ἀδίκως κατηγοροῦντες.

Of persons treating one another ill. Isoc. *Philip.* (5). 38: ἐπὴν δὲ κακῶς ἀλλήλους διαθῶσιν, οὐδενὸς διαλύοντος αὐτοὶ διέστησαν.

Of a soldier who had cut off his own nose and ears, and otherwise ill treated himself, in order to deceive the enemy. Herod. 3. 156: οὐκ ἐστι οὗτος ἀνήρ, ὅτι μὴ σύ, τῷ ἐστι δύναμις τοσαύτη ἐμὲ δὴ ὧδε διαθεῖναι. *Ibid.*: φὰς διὰ τοὺς πολιορκεομένους σεαυτὸν ἀνηκέστως διαθεῖναι. Cf. Xen. *Anab.* 1. 1. 5 and Plat. *Legg.* 728 B.

c) The passive is also used in this sense, to be *handled, treated*. Thuc. 6. 57: οὐ ῥᾳδίως διετέθη, "he was not gently handled." Isoc. *Aig.* (19). 29: ἐγὼ μὲν γὰρ οὕτω κακῶς διετέθην.

4. *To dispose a person so and so to someone or something* (πρός τινα or τι), *to give one an inclination or tendency to a certain action or sentiment*. Isoc. *Philip.* (5). 80: ὅταν οὕτω διαθῇς τοὺς Ἕλληνας, ὥσπερ ὁρᾷς Λακε-δαιμονίους τε πρὸς τοὺς αὐτῶν βασιλέας. Dem. *De cor.* (18). 29: οὕτω διαθεὶς ὁ Φίλιππος τὰς πόλεις πρὸς ἀλλήλας.

Also in passive *to be disposed* in a certain manner to someone or something (πρός τινα, τι).

Of Ceres being kindly disposed toward men. Isoc. *Paneg.* (4). 29: Δήμητρος . . . . πρὸς τοὺς προγόνους ἡμῶν εὐμενῶς διατεθείσης ἐκ τῶν εὐερ-γεσιῶν; cf. *id.* 43.

Isoc. *Epist.* 7. 13: πρὸ πολλοῦ ἂν οἰκείως (σὲ) διατεθῆναι πρὸς ἡμᾶς. Plat. *Symp.* 207 C: *to be in love*, ἐρωτικῶς.

II. Middle: *To make a disposition for oneself, to dispose of one's own, to arrange according to one's own desires, to make a disposition, settlement, or agreement in one's own interest.*

1. In general, *to dispose of, arrange or manage to suit oneself.*

Of a daughter, Xen. *Cyr.* 5. 2. 7: τὴν δὲ θυγατέρα ταύτην ἐπιτρέπω διαθέσθαι, ὅπως ἂν σὺ βούλῃ.

Of beauty and wisdom. Xen. *Mem.* 1. 6. 13: παρ' ἡμῖν νομίζεται τὴν ὥραν καὶ τὴν σοφίαν ὁμοίως μὲν καλὸν, ὁμοίως δὲ αἰσχρὸν διατίθεσθαι εἶναι.

Of hopes; i. e., the matter of hope. Eurip. *Ion.* 866:[1] φροῦδαι δ' ἐλπίδες, ἃς διαθέσθαι.

Of the treatment of bodies or persons. Isoc. *Panath.* (12). 140: μηδ' ἀνέξονται φονὴν τῶν τὰ μὲν σώματα τὰ σφέτερ' αὐτῶν ἐπονειδίστως διαθεμένων, συμβουλεύειν δὲ τοῖς ἄλλοις ἀξιούντων ("nor endure the voice of those treating their own bodies shamefully, yet planning to give advice to others").

To dispose of one's leisure, Chilo (656 B. C.) in Diog. Laert. 1. 69: σχολὴν εὖ διαθέσθαι.

2. *To dispose oneself* in a certain manner toward, *act in a certain way toward, conduct oneself.*

Of the way in which we conduct ourselves toward, or the attitude we assume to beauty and virtue. Isoc. *Laud. Hel.* (10). 55: γνοίη δ' ἂν τις κἀκεῖθεν ὅσον διαφέρει τῶν ὄντων, ἐξ ὧν αὐτοὶ διατιθέμεθα πρὸς ἕκαστον αὐτῶν.

3. *To display for sale, to dispose of by sale, to sell.*

a) *To expose for sale,* Herod 1. 1. 1; of the Phoenicians setting out their wares for sale on their arrival at Argos: ἀπικομένους δὲ τοὺς Φοίνικας ἐς δὴ τὸ Ἄργος τοῦτο διατίθεσθαι τὸν φόρτον.

b) *To dispose of by sale. Id.* 1. 1. 194: ἐπεὰν ὦν ἀπίκωνται πλώοντες ἐς τὴν Βαβυλῶνα καὶ διαθέωνται τὸν φόρτον. Xen. *Hellen.* 4. 5. 8: τὰ αἰχμάλωτα διετίθετο; cf. 4. 6. 6; Xen. *Anab.* 7. 3. 10; Plat. *Legg.* 849 D; Xen. *Anab.* 7. 3. 5 and 7. 4. 2.

4. *To export.* Isoc. *Paneg.* 42: Ἔτι δὲ τὴν χώραν οὐκ αὐτάρκη κεκτημένων ἑκάστων, ἀλλὰ τὰ μὲν ἐλλείπουσαν, τὰ δὲ πλείω τῶν ἱκανῶν φέρουσαν, καὶ πολλῆς ἀπορίας οὔσης τὰ μὲν ὅπου χρὴ διαθέσθαι, τὰ δ' ὁπόθεν εἰσαγαγέσθαι.

5. *To dispose of one's property according to his will, to make dispositions of it, to devise, to bequeath, to make a will.*

---

[1] Bayfield (London, 1889) says: "The compound διατίθημι is elsewhere found only in prose, excepting Ar. *Av.* 439." It is very rare in poetry, but it is found also in *Hymn Ap.* 254 and 294, and in Timon Fr. 42. 3 (Diels, *Poet. Gr.*); cf. Diog. Laert. 8. 67.

a) To bequeath, to leave something by will. Isae. *De Nicost.* (4). 4: περὶ δὲ τοῦ κλήρου μόνου διαφέροντο οὐδὲν ἂν ἔδει ὑμᾶς σκέψασθαι ἀλλ' εἰ τι διέθετο. *Id. De Apollod.* (7). 1: εἴ τις τελευτήσειν μέλλων διέθετο, εἴ τι πάθοι, τὴν οὐσίαν ἑτέρῳ καὶ ταῦτ' ἐν γράμμασι κατέθετο παρά τισι σημηνάμενος. See also Isoc. *Aig.* (19). 43; Plato 922 ff.; and "Concordance" in this dissertation.

b) *To make a will.* Used in this signification with or without διαθήκην or διαθήκας.

Isaeus *De Arist.* (10). 10: οὐδ' εἰ διέθεντο προσῆκεν αὐτῷ τούτων τῶν χρημάτων κληρονομῆσαι, "not even if they did make wills," etc. Lys. 19. 39: Κόνωνος θάνατος καὶ αἱ διαθῆκαι, ἃς διέθετο ἐν Κύπρῳ.

Of dying *intestate*, Isae. *De Apollod.* (7). 19: ἐὰν ἀδελφὸς ὁμοπάτωρ ἄπαις τελευτήσῃ καὶ μὴ διαθέμενος; cf. 8. 31; Arist. *Pol.* 2. 9: ἢν ἀποθάνῃ μὴ διαθέμενος.

The *devisor, testator,* ὁ διαθέμενος. Isaeus *De Cleon.* (1). 26: τὰς διαθήκας ἀξιοῦσιν εἶναι κυρίας ἃς ὁμολογοῦσι μηδ' αὐτὸν τὸν διαθέμενον ὀρθῶς ἔχειν ἡγεῖσθαι.

See also "Concordance," chap. ii.

6. *To dispose for one's own interest, to make an arrangement or settlement for oneself in which another person or persons are necessarily involved,* and to which as a consequence the second party agrees (otherwise no *settlement* could be made); and so *to settle the terms of* a dispute or quarrel, etc., *to make a covenant;* not used, like συντίθεμαι, of an ordinary contract or bargain, but of a more dignified compact, where usually one party *lays down* or *disposes* the terms, and the other accepts them with all conditions and binds himself, by an oath or solemn promise, to abide by them.

a) *To arrange a settlement with* someone, *to come to an agreement* by means of a *disposition or arrangement* of points in dispute, to *settle mutually.*[1]

Xen. *Mem.* 2. 6. 23: δύνανται δὲ καὶ τὴν ἔριν οὐ μόνον ἀλύπως ἀλλὰ καὶ συμφερόντως ἀλλήλοις διατίθεσθαι. Socrates is here speaking of the "beautiful and good" among mankind (or, as we say, the "elite"). These, because of their excellent character and nobility, can *lay down* terms which the other party not only accepts without trouble, but which are advantageous to both sides. If no more than a simple agreement had been meant here, the word συντίθεσθαι would doubtless

---

[1] Cf. the use of *dispose* in Shakespeare: "'She had disposed with Caesar;'" i. e., bargained or made terms with.

have been used. Cf. Appian *Civ.* 2. 8, where the word is used of making an arrangement with tormenting creditors: διαθέμενος δὲ τοὺς ἐνοχλοῦντας ὡς ἐδύνατο.

Cf. Plat. *Legg.* 834 A: διαθεμένους αὖ περὶ τούτων νόμους. Cremer says that this phrase does not simply correspond with νόμους τιθέναι, to *institute laws*, or νόμους τιθέσθαι, *to give laws for oneself or the state.* He says this is the only recognized passage in classic Greek where it occurs, and here it means *to harmonize laws.*

b) *To make a covenant*; i. e., a solemn compact in which one party lays down the terms and the other agrees to them and binds himself by oath. This agreement is mutual, but in a sense one-sided. It may be used with or without διαθήκην.

Aristoph. *Av.* 440 ff.: ΠΕΙ. ἢν μὴ διάθωνται γ᾽ οἵδε διαθήκην ἐμοὶ ἥνπερ ὁ πίθηκος τῇ γυναικὶ διέθετο, ὁ μαχαιροποιός, μήτε δάκνειν τούτους ἐμὲ μητ᾽ ὀρχίπεδ᾽ ἕλκειν μήτ᾽ ὀρύττειν . . . . ΧΟΡ. διατίθεμαι ᾽γώ. ΠΕΙ. κατόμοσόν νυν ταῦτά μοι. ΧΟΡ. ὄμνυμ᾽ . . , . ὡς τὰς σπονδὰς οὐ μὴ πρότερον παραβῶμεν.

From a study of the above citations it will appear that in the middle voice the meanings are all very closely allied. There is always a *disposition, laying-down*, or *setting-forth in order* of something in one's own interests, and then the idea of a second party being affected or involved, on whose course often the completion of the act depends; e. g., in the most common meaning, *to dispose of one's property by will*, the one party makes dispositions which affect another party, and which do not have complete fulfilment without the concurrence of the second party. Here the idea of agreement is usually remote, but in some instances it becomes quite evident. In No. 3—*to dispose of by sale*— one party lays down his wares in order, or displays them, and no completion of sale is made without the concurrence of a second party. In this sense our word is not a mere equivalent of πωλέω. In No. 6 this phase of the use becomes most evident and essential.

CHAPTER IV

ΔΙΑΘΗΚΗ

The significations of the noun διαθήκη correspond in the main to those of the middle voice of its cognate verb διατίθημι, discussed in the previous chapter. The sense of arrangement or disposition is always present in a greater or less degree, together with some idea of mutuality. It is not a common word. Out of 212 writers examined only nine use it, although there are several others who use διατίθεμαι in such a way as to imply the use of διαθήκη. Accordingly we find that this term is always used in a dignified sense, referring to a solemn transaction originally connected with religious rites and obligations.

1. *Arrangements or dispositions*[1] in a general sense, used in the plural number and referring to the arrangements or dispositions a person makes with reference to his property in view of death. This specific connotation is probably not necessary, but the context of the passages in which the word is found indicates that it has such reference in these instances. It is quite probable that, if we had more instances of its use, we should find it employed with reference to other things than distribution of property in view of death.

Isae. 1. 24: εἰ γὰρ δή, ὦ ἄνδρες, ὡς οὗτοί φασιν, ἐν ταῖς νῦν γεγραμμέναις διαθήκαις ἔδωκεν αὐτοῖς τὴν οὐσίαν ("if by means of *these written dispositions* he gave them his property").

Id. 4. 13: τοῦ δὲ συμβαίνοντός ἐστι καὶ γεγραμματεῖον ἀλλαγῆναι καὶ τἀναντία ταῖς τεθνῶτος διαθήκαις μεταγραφῆναι. Here ταῖς διαθήκαις does not refer to the document as a whole, but to the arrangements or dispositions contained in the document. It cannot be translated here "will" or "testament."

Id. 9. 5: ἐπειδὴ δ' ἐπεδήμησα ἐγὼ καὶ ᾐσθόμην καρπομένους τούτους τὰ ἐκείνου, ὁ δὲ υἱὸς αὐτοῦ ποιηθείη ὑπὸ 'Αστυφίλου, καὶ τούτων διαθήκας καταλίποι παρὰ 'Ιεροκλεῖ.

2. *Arrangements* or *dispositions* which a person makes with reference to his property to take effect at his death, the terms or provisions of a will. In this sense the plural is used, but the word can be translated by "will" or "testament" in the singular. However, the writer has in

---

[1] No English word expresses the exact sense of διαθήκη. These words are used for lack of a better term.

mind the several dispositions or provisions contained in the will, and not the instrument as a whole in a technical sense.

The fact that in a considerable majority (120 out of 210 examined) of instances in which reference is made to testamentary dispositions, the plural (διαθῆκαι) is used, has led writers on Greek wills to take for granted that there is no difference of use between the singular and the plural of this word.

Lys. 19. 39: ὁ γὰρ Κόνωνος θάνατος καὶ αἱ διαθῆκαι ἃς διέθετο ἐν Κύπρῳ, σαφῶς ἐδήλωσαν ὅτι πολλοστὸν μέρος ἦν τὰ χρήματα ὧν ὑμεῖς προσεδοκᾶτε.

Isae. 2. 14: ἐμὲ ποιεῖται, οὐκ ἐν διαθήκαις γράψας μέλλων ἀποθνήσκειν.

Demos. 27. 14: δῆλον τοίνυν ἐστὶν οὐδὲν ἧττον τὸ πλῆθος τῶν καταλει-φθέντων, καίπερ ἀφανιζόντων τούτων τὴν οὐσίαν ἐκ τῶν διαθηκῶν,ἐξ ὧν τοσαῦτα χρήματ' ἀλλήλοις φασὶ δοθῆναι.

3. The *disposition* or *arrangement* which a man makes with reference to his property in view of death. The word is here used in the singular number to denote the instrument as a whole—a Greek will or testament in the legal or technical sense. As the Greek testament does not correspond in all respects to ours, it will be necessary to discuss its characteristics in detail. This will be done in the second part of this dissertation.

Aristoph. *Vesp.* 584:

κἂν ἀποθνήσκων ὁ πατήρ τῳ δῷ καταλείπων παῖδ' ἐπίκληρον
κλάειν ἡμεῖς μακρὰ τὴν κεφαλὴν εἰπόντες τῇ διαθήκῃ
καὶ τῇ κόγχῃ τῇ πάνυ σεμνῶς τοῖς σημείοισιν ἐπούσῃ,
ἔδομεν ταύτην ὅστις ἂν ἡμᾶς ἀντιβολήσας ἀναπείσῃ.

Cf. *ibid.* 589.

Demos. 46. 25: ἄκυρος μὲν ἡ διαθήκη ἐστιν, ἥν φασιν οὗτοι τὸν πατέρα καταλιπεῖν, ... ἀντίγραφά ἐστι τῆς διαθήκης τῆς Πασίωνος · cf. *id.* 45. 21.

Plato 923 C: ὃς ἂν διαθήκην γράφῃ τὰ αὑτοῦ διατιθέμενος.

4. *A disposition of relations between two parties, where one party lays down the conditions which the other accepts.* This is a "one-sided" transaction, in so far as one party does all the disposing; but, as another party is necessarily involved, and his consent is necessary to a settlement, it becomes to a certain extent a mutual agreement. διαθήκη is not used, like συνθήκη, of an ordinary bargain or contract, but of a more dignified and solemn compact or covenant.[1] In the case of συνθήκη the convention is entirely mutual, both parties being on an equality and having an equal part in arranging the terms.

---

[1] This signification is more fully illustrated by the use of διατίθεμαι (chap iii, 6).

a) An agreement, or *settlement*, arrived at by means of a disposition
or arrangement of points in dispute, a *mutual settlement*.

Isae. 6. 23: εἰδότες δ' οἱ ἀναγκαῖοι ὅτι ἐξ ἐκείνου μὲν οὐκ ἂν ἔτι γένοιντο
παῖδες ταύτην τὴν ἡλικίαν ἔχοντος, φανήσοιντο δ' ἄλλῳ τινὶ τρόπῳ, καὶ ἐκ τούτων
ἔσοιντο ἔτι μείζους διαφοραί, ἔπειθον, ὦ ἄνδρες, τὸν Φιλοκτήμονα ἐᾶσαι εἰσαγαγεῖν τοῦτον τὸν παῖδα ἐφ' οἷς ἐζήτει ὁ Εὐκτήμων, χωρίον ἓν δόντα. (24) καὶ
ὁ Φιλοκτήμων αἰσχυνόμενος μὲν ἐπὶ τῇ τοῦ πατρὸς ἀνοίᾳ, ἀπορῶν δ' ὅ τι χρή-
σαιτο τῷ παρόντι κακῷ οὐκ ἀντέλεγεν οὐδέν. ὁμολογηθέντων δὲ τούτων καὶ
εἰσαχθέντος τοῦ παιδὸς ἐπὶ τούτοις ἀπηλλάγη τῆς γυναικὸς ὁ Εὐκτήμων, καὶ ἐπ-
εδείξατο ὅτι οὐ παίδων ἕνεκα ἐγάμει, ἀλλ' ἵνα τοῦτον εἰσαγάγοι. . . . . (27) μετὰ
ταῦτα τοίνυν ὁ Φιλοκτήμων τριηραρχῶν περὶ Χίον ἀποθνήσκει ὑπὸ τῶν πολεμίων·
ὁ δ' Εὐκτήμων ὕστερον χρόνῳ πρὸς τοὺς κηδεστὰς εἶπεν ὅτι βούλοιτο τὰ πρὸς
τὸν υἱόν οἱ πεπραγμένα γράψας καταθέσθαι. καὶ ὁ μὲν Φανόστρατος ἐκπλεῖν
ἔμελλε τριηραρχῶν μετὰ Τιμοθέου, καὶ ἡ ναῦς αὐτῷ ἐξώρμει Μουνυχίασι, καὶ ὁ
κηδεστὴς Χαιρέας παρὼν συναπέστελλεν αὐτόν· ὁ δ' Εὐκτήμων παραλαβών
τινας ἧκεν οὗ ἐξώρμει ἡ ναῦς, καὶ γράψας διαθήκην, ἐφ' οἷς εἰσήγαγε τὸν παῖδα,
κατατίθεται μετὰ τούτων παρὰ Πυθοδώρῳ Κηφισεῖ, προσήκοντι αὐτῷ. . . . .
(29) Κειμένου δὲ τοῦ γραμματείου σχεδὸν δύ' ἔτη καὶ τοῦ Χαιρέου τετελευτηκότος, ὑποπεπτωκότες οἶδε τῇ ἀνθρώπῳ, καὶ ὁρῶντες ἀπολλύμενον τὸν οἶκον
καὶ τὸ γῆρας καὶ τὴν ἄνοιαν τοῦ Εὐκτήμονος, ὅτι εἴη αὐτοῖς ἱκανὴ ἀφορμή,
συνεπιτίθενται. (30) καὶ πρῶτον μὲν πείθουσι τὸν Εὐκτήμονα τὴν μὲν διαθήκην
ἀνελεῖν ὡς οὐ χρησίμην οὖσαν τοῖς παισί· τῆς γὰρ φανερᾶς οὐσίας οὐδένα κύριον
ἔσεσθαι τελευτήσαντος Εὐκτήμονος ἄλλον ἢ τὰς θυγατέρας καὶ τοὺς ἐκ τούτων
γεγονότας· εἰ δὲ ἀποδόμενός τι τῶν ὄντων ἀργύριον καταλίποι τοῦτο βεβαίως
ἕξειν αὐτούς. (31) ἀκούσας δ' ὁ Εὐκτήμων εὐθὺς ἀπῄτει τὸν Πυθόδωρον τὸ
γραμματεῖον, καὶ προσεκαλέσατο εἰς ἐμφανῶν κατάστασιν. καταστάντος δὲ
ἐκείνου πρὸς τὸν ἄρχοντα, ἔλεγεν ὅτι βούλοιτ' ἀνελέσθαι τὴν διαθήκην. (32)
ἐπειδὴ δ' ὁ Πυθόδωρος ἐκείνῳ μὲν καὶ τῷ Φανοστράτῳ παρόντι ὡμολόγει ἀναιρεῖν,
τοῦ δὲ Χαιρέου τοῦ συγκαταθεμένου θυγάτηρ ἦν μία, ἧς ἐπειδὴ κύριος κατασταίη,
τότε ἠξίου ἀνελεῖν, καὶ ὁ ἄρχων οὕτως ἐγίγνωσκε, διομολογησάμενος ὁ Εὐκτήμων
ἐναντίον τοῦ ἄρχοντος καὶ τῶν παρέδρων καὶ ποιησάμενος πολλοὺς μάρτυρας ὡς
οὐκέτ' αὐτῷ κέοιτο ἡ διαθήκη, ᾤχετο ἀπιών.

In order to understand the significance of διαθήκη in these passages,
we must know something of the context. Briefly the story is as follows:

Euctemon, a wealthy Athenian, died at the age of ninety-six. By his
wife he had had three sons and two daughters. One of his sons, Philoctemon, outlived the other two, but all three died before their father. Both
daughters survived him. One was a widow, her husband, Chaereas, having
died seven years before Euctemon, leaving one daughter. The other was
the wife of Phanostratus and had two sons, the eldest of whom, Chaerestratus,

put in a claim to Euctemon's estate, on the ground that he had been adopted by Philoctemon in a will.

Euctemon in his old age had formed an attachment for a woman of ill-repute named Alce, who kept a lodging-house that was owned by him. She gained such an ascendancy over him that he deserted his family and went to live with her. She had two sons, whose reputed father was a freedman named Dion. She finally persuaded the old man to introduce the eldest of her sons into his φρατρία as his son. Philoctemon resisted this, and succeeded in inducing the members of the φρατρία to reject the candidate. Euctemon, enraged, threatened to marry again, and the relatives, fearing further complications, in order to restore peace in the family persuaded Philoctemon to agree to a compromise on terms proposed by Euctemon (ἐφ᾽ οἷς ἐζήτει ὁ Εὐκτή-. μων). Euctemon laid down the terms of an arrangement or settlement with his son Philoctemon, in which, on condition of obtaining Philoctemon's consent to the admission of Alce's boy into his φρατρία, he agreed to give the boy only one farm (χωρίον ἕν). To this arrangement Philoctemon agreed, and the boy was presented again and admitted (§ 24).

Some time afterward Philoctemon was slain in battle, and a considerable time after this, Euctemon told his sons-in-law that he wished to put into writing and deposit for safe-keeping the terms of the arrangement that he had made with his son (τὰ πρὸς τὸν υἱὸν οἱ πεπραγμένα); and when Phanostratus was on the point of setting out on an expedition as trierarch, and Chaereas was with him to see him off, he came to them, bringing some witnesses with him; and having written out a settlement (γράψας διαθήκην), according to the terms of which (ἐφ᾽ οἷς) he had introduced the boy into his φρατρία, he deposited it, in concurrence with them,[1] with Pythodorus, one of his relatives. Thus his sons-in-law, representing his daughters, became parties to the original compromise or agreement that he had made with Philoctemon.

Two years after this, when Euctemon influenced by Alce and her friends, demanded the document from Pythodorus, with a view to destroying it, and summoned him to produce it in court, Pythodorus refused to give it up without the consent of all the contracting parties. Euctemon said that he wished to get it back in order to destroy it. The consent of Phanostratus, who was present, was obtained, and still Pythodorus did not think it right to destroy it without the consent of a legal representative of the deceased Chaereas, who had been one of the depositors.[2]

This instrument served the purpose of a will as well as that of a compact. This explains the orator's words in § 28. He argues that, if Alce's boy were the legitimate son of Euctemon, it would not have been necessary for a διαθήκη to have been made in order that he might

[1] κατατίθεται μετὰ τούτων; cf. 32. 3, τοῦ δὲ Χαιρέου τοῦ συγκαταθεμένου.
[2] τοῦ δὲ Χαιρέου τοῦ συγκαταθεμένου.

have the inheritance, as he would receive it by the laws of intestate succession.[1] If it had been a mere will, the consent of the sons-in-law would not have been necessary to its revocation.[2] The fact that it was legally a contract explains Pythodorus' refusal to give it up without the consent of all the parties. If it were lost, he was liable to a suit for damages,[3] and from a passage in Demosthenes it appears that it was not safe to intrust it even to a magistrate.[4]

Isae. 4. 12: περὶ μὲν γὰρ τῶν ἄλλων συμβολαίων οὐ πάνυ χάλεπον τοὺς τὰ ψευδῆ μαρτυροῦντας ἐλέγχειν ζῶντος γὰρ καὶ παρόντος τοῦ πράξοντος καταμαρτυροῦσι· περὶ δὲ τῶν διαθηκῶν πῶς ἄν τις γνοίη τοὺς μὴ τἀληθῆ λέγοντας;

Id. 10. 10: παιδὸς γὰρ οὐκ ἔξεστι διαθήκην γενέσθαι· ὁ γὰρ νόμος διαρρήδην κωλύει παιδὶ μὴ ἐξεῖναι συμβάλλειν μηδὲ γυναικὶ πέρα μεδίμνου κριθῶν.

In these passages Isaeus classes διαθῆκαι among συμβόλαια. In an evident attempt to avoid the conclusion reached by some early writers[5] on Greek testamentary law, that the Athenians considered the testament to be a "contract," later authorities[6] have given far-fetched interpretations of this word. Isaeus himself uses it in another connection in 5. 33. A synopsis of the context is as follows:

Diceogenes and Leochares asked us to delay this trial, when we were bringing it on some time ago, and to refer the matter to arbitrators. We agreed. Two arbitrators were appointed by each side, and we both swore to abide by their decision. After learning the facts, the two arbitrators appointed by me wished to render sentence, but the two appointed by Leochares refused. Now, one of them was related to him, and was my personal enemy and opponent ἐξ ἑτέρων συμβολαίων.

[1] Some writers have had difficulty with this document, because they take the word διαθήκη here to mean simply "testament," as the orator seems to refer to it as such in § 28. The confusion has arisen from not recognizing the fact that the word διαθήκη had more meaning to Isaeus than "testament" has to us. The senses of "testament" and "compact" were so closely allied that the same word could be used for both, and the orator could have either or both in mind as suited his argument. In fact, we have no one word that exactly expresses the idea conveyed by διαθήκη to the Greeks.

[2] See Part II, 4.   [3] Dem. 33. 17, 38; cf. Bonner, p. 66.   [4] Dem. 45. 57.

[5] Bunsen, *De iure hereditario Atheniensium* (1813), p. 53; Gans, *Das Erbrecht in weltgeschichtlicher Entwickelung* (1824), p, 384.

[6] Schulin, *Das griechische Testament*, p. 8, n. 6, "Rechtsgeschäft;" Beauchet II, p. 364, "tout acte juridique;" III, p. 671, "acte en général;" Meier-Schömann-Lipsius, pp. 564, 595. "Geschäftsurkunde." Schulin and Beauchet give no authority for their opinion; Lipsius appeals only to an obscure article in Harpocration on δόσις (δόσις: ἰδίως λέγεται παρὰ τοῖς ῥήτορσι συμβόλαιον γραφόμενον ὅταν τις τὰ αὑτοῦ διδῷ τινὶ διὰ τῶν ἀρχόντων, ὡς παρὰ Δεινάρχῳ)

While the signification "contract" is doubtless too restricted to include all uses of the term, it is certainly a greater error to eliminate all elements of mutuality from it and make it so general as "legal transaction" (*Rechtsgeschäft, tout acte juridique*) or "instrument" (*Geschäftsurkunde*). In its widest signification it is used to mean *covenant, engagement, dealings,* and undoubtedly always refers to some relation or relations between two parties.[1]

Cf. Eurip. *Ion.* 411: ὦ πότνια Φοίβου μῆτερ, εἰ γὰρ αἰσίως | ἔλθοιμεν. ἅ τε τῶν συμβόλαια πρόσθεν ἦν | ἐς παῖδα τὸν σόν, μεταπέσοι βελτίονα.

Plut. *Alex.* 30: τί γὰρ εὐπρεπὲς ἀνδρὶ νέῳ πρὸς ἐχθροῦ γυναῖκα συμβόλαιον.

Plato also classes διαθῆκαι among συμβόλαια: *Legg.* 922 A: τὰ μὲν δὴ μέγιστα τῶν συμβολαίων, ὅσα πρὸς ἀλλήλους ἄνθρωποι συμβάλλουσι, πλήν γε ὀρφανικῶν καὶ τῆς τῶν ἐπιτρόπων ἐπιμελείας τῶν ὀρφανῶν, σχεδὸν ἡμῖν διατέτακται· ταῦτα δὲ δὴ μετὰ τὰ νῦν εἰρημένα ἀναγκαῖον ἀμῶς'γέ πως τάξασθαι. τούτων δὲ ἀρχαὶ πάντων αἵ τε τῶν τελευτᾶν μελλόντων ἐπιθυμίαι τῆς διαθέσεως αἵ τε τῶν μηδὲν τὸ παράπαν διαθεμένων τύχαι· . . . . πολλὰ γὰρ ἕκαστοι καὶ διάφορα ἀλλήλων καὶ ἐναντία τιθεῖντ' ἂν τοῖς τε νόμοις καὶ τοῖς τῶν ζώντων ἤθεσι καὶ τοῖς αὐτῶν τοῖς ἔμπροσθεν, πρὶν διατίθεσθαι μέλλειν, εἴ τις ἐξουσίαν δώσει ἁπλῶς οὕτω κυρίαν εἶναι διαθήκην, ἣν ἄν τις διαθῆται ὁπωσοῦν ἔχων πρὸς τῷ τοῦ βίου τέλει.

Plato here uses the term in its widest sense of "dealings between man and man." He has been giving (913–21) regulations with regard to *meum et tuum,* disputed ownership, slaves, freedmen, buying and selling, letting and hiring. He then says (922 A): "The greater part of the συμβολαίων which men συμβάλλουσι with one another have been regulated by us;" and then goes on to give regulations with regard to διαθῆκαι.

Cf. *Rep.* I. 333 A: συμβόλαια δὲ λέγεις κοινωνήματα, ἤ τι ἄλλο; κοινωνήματα δῆτα. "'By contracts do you mean partnerships.' The more general word is substituted for the sake of extending the analogy."[2]

b) *A disposition or settlement of relations between two parties,* wherein one party lays down the conditions, and the other accepts them and binds himself by an oath or solemn promise to keep them; a settlement, arrangement, compact, covenant. This signification is quite fully illustrated by the use of διατίθεμαι (See chap. iii, 6).

---

[1]Compare the verb συμβάλλειν, which always expresses the idea of duality of action.

[2]Jowett III, p. 19.

Aristoph. *Av.* 435–61:

ΕΠ. ἄγε δὴ σὺ καὶ σὺ μὲν πάλιν τὴν πανοπλίαν   435
    ταύτην λάβοντε κρεμάσατον τύχἀγαθῇ
    ἐς τὸν ἰπνὸν εἴσω πλησίον τοὐπιστάτου
    σὺ δὲ τοὐσδ' ἐφ' οἶστισιν λόγοις ξυνέλεξ' ἐγὼ
    φράσον, δίδαξον. ΠΕ. μὰ τὸν Ἀπόλλω 'γὼ μὲν οὔ,
    ἢν μὴ διάθωνταί γ' οἵδε διαθήκην ἐμοὶ   440
    ἥνπερ ὁ πίθηκος τῇ γυναικὶ διέθετο,
    ὁ μαχαιροποιός, μήτε δάκνειν τούτους ἐμὲ
    μήτ' ὀρχίπεδ' ἕλκειν μήτ' ὀρύττειν—ΧΟ. οὔτι που
    τόνδ'; οὐδαμῶς. ΠΕ. οὐκ, ἀλλὰ τὠφθαλμὼ λέγω.
ΧΟ. διατίθεμαι 'γω. ΠΕ. κατόμοσόν νυν ταῦτά μοι.   445

. . . .

ΧΟ. ὄμνυμ' ἐπὶ τούτοις, ...

. . . .

ἀλλ' ἐφ' ὅτῳπερ πράγματι ἥκεις τὴν σὴν γνώμην ἀναπείσας   460
λέγε θαρρήσας, ὡς τὰς σπονδὰς οὐ μὴ πρότεροι παραβῶμεν.

This reference (vs. 440) is given by the lexicons and cited by many
writers for the meaning "agreement," or "covenant." But as sufficient context has never been given, and a recent writer[1] has ventured
the assertion that "it is not clear," I have given a full quotation. In
brief, the story is as follows:

Two old men of Athens, Euelpides and Peisthetaerus, becoming wearied
with the disputes, contentions, and lawsuits at home, decide to leave Athens
and try to find a more congenial city where they may enjoy "the simple life."
They have heard a great deal of Epops, king of the birds, who was once a
man and had married an Athenian woman; and they determine to go to his
kingdom and inquire of the birds where they can find such a city as they
desire. They suppose that the birds will know, because of the fact that they
travel more than any other people.

When they arrive in the bird's kingdom and consult King Epops, he men-
tions several cities; but they reject them all for various reasons. Then he
tells them of the happiness of living in his own kingdom, and they are greatly
pleased with the simple life of the birds. Peisthetaerus, who is a shrewd old
fellow, suggests a scheme to improve it, and to make the birds superior to
men and gods. Epops summons the birds together, that Peisthetaerus may
address them and explain to them his scheme. They assemble in a great
crowd at the call of the nightingale; but, on seeing the men, they become
greatly disturbed, and, supposing that Epops has betrayed them into the
hands of their enemies, they draw themselves up in battle array, and prepare

[1] Ramsay, p. 362.

to rush upon the men and tear them to pieces. The men are greatly alarmed, and hastily snatch up Epops' kitchen utensils, and, armed with pots, pans, and spits, prepare to make a stout resistance. Hereupon Epops interposes, addresses the birds, and pleads for his guests, whom he calls his wife's relatives. He tells the birds that they are men of great wisdom and friendly to his kingdom, and that they have come because they have fallen in love with the birds' way of life and want to live among them. The birds assume a more peaceful attitude, give back a little, and consent to listen to Peisthetaerus. Epops then addresses the two men: "Come, then, you and you; take this panoply and hang it up again for good luck in the kitchen beside the caldron; and do you (motioning to Peisthetaerus) speak to these (pointing to the birds) and explain to them the reasons why I assembled them." Peisthetaerus answers: "Not I, by Apollo, unless they make a covenant (διάθωνται διαθήκην) with me such as that monkey, the sword-maker, made (διέθετο) with his wife, not to bite me nor drag me by the orchipeda nor poke "——

Chorus of Birds: "You don't mean the——? Surely not.
Peisthetaerus: "No, but I mean my eyes."
The Birds: "I covenant" (διατίθεμαι).
Peisthetaerus: "Swear it then."
The Birds: "I swear on these conditions . . . . So, whatever you have come to say, speak boldly, for I will not be the first to break the treaty" (τὰς σπονδάς).[1]

This is evidently not a mere bargain or contract, but a solemn compact or covenant, ratified by an oath. Regarding the reference to the swordmaker and his wife, Droysen says:

According to the Scholiast, this is Panaetius. He was a great simpleton and a little man. He had a large wife, who sorely henpecked him. Having

[1] For the sake of comparison, I subjoin a metrical version of vss. 435 ff. by B. H. Kennedy (London, 1874):

Ep. "Now you and you this panoply take back
And hang it up in prospect of good luck
Within the kitchen by the plate-rack's side.
And you, sir, make the statement which to hear
I summoned these: expound."

Pe. "Not I, by Apollo,
Unless they make the covenant with me
Which with his wife that ape the swordwright made
That they won't bite or worry me, in short,
Won't scratch my eyes out."

Cho. "Good: I covenant."

Pe. "Then swear it."

Cho. "Well I swear: if I am faithful
Then by the votes of all the judges here
And all the spectators the first prize be mine."

Pe. "Accepted."

Cho. "But if I transgress the oath
Then by one judge's casting vote—I win.
. . . .
So whatever be the thing you with full conviction bring
Let it now be boldly spoken, for our truce will not be broken."

J. H. Frere (London, 1886) renders vs. 440: "Unless they agree to an armistice [in a note he calls it "a formal treaty of peace"], such as the little baboon, our neighbor, concluded with his wife;" vs. 461: "The birds will adhere to the truce that we made."

been once caught by him committing adultery, she beat him till he concluded the above-mentioned treaty.

The big wife laid down the terms, and the little husband agreed to them. But, aside from this reference, the passage is quite clear. Peisthetaerus will not put down his weapons until the birds agree to make a covenant with him, the terms of which he lays down. There is no doubt of the reading διαθήκην here. The MSS give no other word, and no other word[1] would suit the context. We cannot say διάθωνται συνθήκην. It is referred to again in the next line by the word διέθετο; and in the next line, when the chorus answer, they say διατίθεμαι.

I do not think that it would be possible to find a more definite and explicit example of the meaning of a word than that of διαθήκην in this passage. If there were no other occurrence of it in the language, this would be sufficient to establish clearly the signification of *solemn compact*, or *covenant*.

[1] See Ramsay, p. 362, note.

PART SECOND

THE HISTORICAL STUDY: THE GREEK WILL

CHAPTER V

ORIGIN AND DEVELOPMENT

The earliest reference in Greek literature to a bequest is found in
Homer's *Iliad* ii. 106, 107. The story of Agamemnon's scepter is here
given (106–8). It was made by Hephaestus, who presented it to Zeus.
Zeus gave it to Hermes, Hermes to Pelops, and Pelops to Atreus.
Atreus, when dying, left it to Thyestes, and he in turn left it to
Agamemnon.[1] That this is not simple hereditary succession would seem
to be evident from the fact that Atreus, who had sons, left it to his
brother Thyestes, and Thyestes, who also had sons, left it to his nephew
Agamemnon. The simple narrative reads as if the men in question had
a right to dispose of it as they pleased, and did so.

Again in book xvii, lines 196, 197, reference is made to a bequest
of the armor of Peleus to his son Achilles.[2] This is not so clear, and
might be regarded as a *donatio mortis causa;* but the fact that such
committal is mentioned seems to be an indication that the son was not
looked upon as necessarily a universal heir to his father's property.

In Sophocles *Trachiniae* Deianeira is made to say that, when Hercules was going from home on his last journey, he left in the house an
old tablet inscribed with συνθήματα that he had never explained to her
before. He had always before gone off as if to conquer, not to die;

[1] Ἀτρεὺς δὲ θνῄσκων ἔλιπεν πολύαρνι Θυέστῃ,
αὐτὰρ ὁ αὖτε Θυέστ' Ἀγαμέμνονι λεῖπε φορῆναι.

The word ἔδωκε is used of the transfer between the gods and from Pelops, a demi-
god, to his son Atreus. Then a form of λείπω is used. λείπω or καταλείπω is used in
the orators as equivalent to διατίθεμαι.

[2] ὁ δ' ἄρα ὧι παιδὶ ὄπασσε
γηράς· ἀλλ' οὐχ υἱὸς ἐν ἔντεσι πατρὸς ἐγήρα.

but he now told her what part of his property she was to take for her dowry, and how he wished his land divided among his sons.[1]

I do not, of course, present this as evidence that Hercules made a will, but it certainly indicates that will-making of such a character as that which is exhibited in the citation was not only known at the time of Sophocles, but was then a matter of history.[2]

A brief Doric testament engraved on a bronze tessera found near Petelia (Strongoli), which cannot be of later date than the year 511 B. C., is preserved in the museum at Naples. It runs as follows: "God. Fortune. Saotis gives to Sicaenia his house and all his other property. Demiurge: Paragoras. Proxenoi: Mincon, Harmoxidamus, Agatharcus, Onatas, Epicurus."[3]

The beneficiary is a woman and is made universal heir. The name of the magistrate being inserted may indicate his co-operation or it may have been put in simply to indicate the year. There were five witnesses

---

[1] Soph. *Trach.* 155–63:

ὁδὸν γὰρ ἦμος ἡ τελευταίαν ἄναξ
ὡρμᾶτ' ἀπ' οἴκων Ἡρακλῆς, τότ' ἐν δόμοις
λείπει παλαιὰν δέλτον ἐγγεγραμμένην·
συνθήμαθ', ἁμοὶ πρόσθεν οὐκ ἔτλη ποτέ
πολλοὺς ἀγῶνας ἐξιών, οὔπω φράσαι,
ἀλλ' ὡς τι δράσων εἷρπε κοὐ θανούμενος.
νῦν δ' ὡς ἔτ' οὐκ ὢν εἶπε μὲν λέχους ὅ τι
χρείη μ' ἑλέσθαι κτῆσιν, εἶπε δ' ἦν τέκνοις
μοῖραν πατρῴας γῆς διαιρετὸν νέμοι,

[2] À propos of the meaning of διαθήκη, the use of the word συνθήματα to denote the contents of this testamentary document is interesting. This word is used as the equivalent of συνθῆκαι in Plat. *Gorg.* 492 C; Xen. *Anab.* 4. 6. 20, *Hell.* 5. 4. 6; Hdt. 5. 74; 6. 121; Thuc. 4. 6. 7; 6. 61, etc.; Plut. *Amil.* 19; Hdn. 2. 13. In Hdt. 8. 7 and Thuc. 4. 12 it means *a preconcerted signal;* in Xen. *Anab.* 1. 8. 16, *a watchword, password.*

[3] *CIG.* 4; Roehl, *Inscr. ant.*, No. 544; Cauer, *Dilectus*, 2d ed. No. 274; Roberts, Intro., p. 304; Schulin, p. 44; Kaibel, No. 636 (with facsimile); *IJG.*, 2d Series I, p. 59. The text is as follows:

θεὸς· τύχα. Σάοτις δίδ-
οτι Σικαινίαι τὰν ϝοι-
κίαν καὶ τἆλλα πάντ-
α. Δαμιοργὸς Παραγόρ-
ας. Πρόξενοι Μίνκον,
Ἀρμοξίδαμος, Ἀγάθαρ-
χος, Ὀνάτας, Ἐπίκορ
ος.

For the name Σάοτις cf. *CIG.* II. 1247, 2496. Hesychius, Πρόξενοι· μαρτυρεῖ cf. Hdt. 6. 57.

whose names are affixed to the instrument. Although from the words used it might be claimed that this document was a *donatio inter vivos*, the universal character of the disposition (τἄλλα πάντα) seems to preclude such an interpretation.

A bronze slab found at Tegea (Piali in Arcadia), and now in the museum at Athens is engraved on both sides with two independent inscriptions, each of which is at once a deposit and a will. One side has been intentionally defaced and replaced by more detailed dispositions on the other side. The inscriptions are in the Arcadian dialect and date from about the beginning of the fifth century. The slab was probably deposited in the temple of Athena Alea, which was burned in 393 B. C. The inscriptions run as follows:

Side A.—To Xouthias, son of Philachaeus, 200 minas. If he himself lives, let him come and take them up; but if he dies, they shall belong to his children, five years after they reach the age of puberty. If there shall be no children, they shall belong to those who have a right to them. The people of Tegea shall decide according to the law.

Side B.—To Xouthias, son of Philachaeus, a deposit, 400 minas of silver. If he lives, let him take them up himself. If he does not live, let his legitimate sons take them five years after they come to puberty. If these do not live, let his legitimate daughters take them. If these do not live, let his illegitimate sons take them. If the illegitimate sons do not live, let the nearest collateral relatives take them. If there is a dispute, the people of Tegea shall decide according to the law.[1]

[1]Roehl, No. 68; Cauer, No. 10; Roberts, No. 257 and p. 357; Schulin, p. 37; *IJG.*, II, p. 60.

A. Ξουθίαι τôι Φιλαχαίο διακάτι-
αι μναî. αἰ κ' αὐτòς εἰ, ἴτο ἀνελέσ-
θο· αἰ δέ κ' ἀποθάνει, τòν τέκνον
ἴμεν ἐπεί κα πέντε ϝέτεα
ℎεβôντι· αἰ δέ κα μὲ γένετα-
ι τέκνα τòν ἐπιδικατôν ἔμεν·
διαγνόμεν δὲ τòς Τεγεάτα[ς]
κα(τ)τòν θεθμόν.

B. Ξουθίαι παρακαθι θ)έκα τôι Φιλαχαίο τετρακάτιαι μναî ἀργύριο. εἰ μ-
έν κα ζόε, αὐτòς ἀνελέσθο· αἰ δέ κ-
α μὲ ζόε, τοὶ υἱοὶ ἀνελόσθο τοὶ γνέ-
σιοι, ἐπεί κα ἐβάσοντι πέντε ϝέτε-
α· εἰ δέ κα ζôντι, ταὶ θυγατέρες
[ά]νελόσθο ταὶ γνέσιαι· εἰ δέ κα μὲ
ζ[ô]ντι, τοὶ νόθοι ἀνελόσθο· εἰ δέ κα
μὲ νόθαι ζôντι, τοὶ σασιστα (sic) πόθικ-
ες ἀνελόσθο· εἰ δέ κ' ανφιλέγοντ(ι, τ-)
οἱ Τεγâται διαγνôντο κα(τ)τòν
θεθμόν.

Roberts says:

The depositor is in both cases the same, Xouthias, son of Philachaeus. The documents cannot, therefore, be more than two or three decades apart; the similarity of the writing also points to the same conclusion. On side A the writing seems to have been purposely defaced, and it was probably intended to be canceled by side B, which was thus later. It is in agreement with this view that we find on A regularly *αί*, on B chiefly *εί*.

Dareste, Haussoullier, and Reinach say: "Nous avons ici un exemple de révocation ou tout au moins de modification d'un testament par un acte ultérieur." These inscriptions seem to indicate a free power of testation. He minutely regulates the succession: (1) legitimate sons; (2) legitimate daughters; (3) bastards; (4) collateral relatives. That the testator was not a native of Tegea is indicated by the last clause of each document. Some authorities think he was a Spartan, and had made his deposit and testament here to escape the more stringent laws of his own country; others, from philological reasons, judge that he was an Achaean.

Aristotle complains of the liberty of bequest as one of the causes of the decay of the Lacedaemonian state, making possible the inequality of holdings of land that existed in his day. He says that, while the law stigmatized the purchase or sale of one's patrimony, it gave him liberty to give or bequeath it.[1]

Plutarch agrees with Aristotle in assigning, as one of the chief causes of the decline of Sparta, the freedom of gift and bequest. He says that a certain Epitadeus, an ephor of the fourth century, having quarreled with his son, had a law adopted "permitting a man to give his house and land to whomsoever he pleased, either during his life or by will after his death." Up to this time the number of houses instituted by Lycurgus had been maintained, and each father had left his estate to his son.[2]

---

[1] Aristot. *Politics* ii. 9: ὠνεῖσθαι μὲν γὰρ ἢ πολεῖν τὴν ὑπάρχουσαν (γῆν) ἐποίησεν οὐ καλόν, ὀρθῶς ποιήσας, διδόναι δὲ καὶ καταλείπειν ἐξουσίαν ἔδωκε τοῖς βουλομένοις.

[2] Plut. *Agis* 5: Ἀρχὴν μὲν οὖν διαφθορὰς καὶ τοῦ νοσεῖν ἔσχε τὰ πράγματα τῶν Λακεδαιμονίων σχεδὸν ἀφ' οὗ τὴν Ἀθηναίων καταλύσαντες ἡγεμονίαν χρησίου τε καὶ ἀργυρίου κατέπλησαν ἑαυτούς. οὐ μὴν ἀλλὰ καὶ τῶν οἴκων ὃν ὁ Λυκοῦργος ὥρισε φυλαττόντων ἀριθμὸν ἐν ταῖς διαδοχαῖς, καὶ πατρὸς παιδὶ τὸν κλῆρον ἀπολείποντος. ἁμῶς γέ πως ἡ τάξις αὕτη καὶ ἰσότης διαμένουσα τὴν πόλιν ἐκ τῶν ἄλλων ἀνέφερεν ἁμαρτημάτων. ἐφόρευσας δέ τις ἀνὴρ δυνατός, αὐθάδης δὲ καὶ χαλεπὸς τὸν τρόπον. Ἐπιτάδευς ὄνομα, πρὸς τὸν υἱὸν αὐτῷ γενομένης διαφορᾶς ῥήτραν ἔγραψεν ἐξεῖναι τὸν οἶκον αὐτοῦ καὶ τὸν κλῆρον ᾧ τις ἐθέλοι καὶ ζῶντα δοῦναι καὶ καταλιπεῖν διατιθέμενον.

Plato in his *Laws* finds fault with the ancient legislators for being too lenient in granting liberty of bequest, and proceeds to suggest stricter rules. He makes the Athenian representative say that "the ancient legislators passed a law to the effect that a man should be permitted to bequeath his property in all respects as he desired."[1] This seems to indicate that the utmost liberty of bequest was allowed in Plato's time, and that this state of affairs had existed for a long time— so long that he could speak of it as "ancient" in his day.

The law of Solon respecting wills, as stated by the orators, was to the effect that a man might bequeath his property as he pleased, if he had no legitimate male children, and was not disqualified by old age, drugs, or disease, influenced by a woman's persuasions, or under duress.[2]

Plutarch, in his life of Solon, says that

he gained credit also by his laws about wills. Before his time these were not permitted, but the money and lands of a deceased person were inherited by his family in all cases. Solon, however, permitted anyone who had no children to leave his property to whom he would, honoring friendship more than nearness of kin, and giving a man absolute power to dispose of his inheritance. Yet, on the other hand, he did not permit legacies to be given without restrictions, but disallowed all that were obtained by the effects of disease or by the administration of drugs to the testator, or by imprisonment and violence or by the solicitations of his wife.[3]

The above citations and inscriptions show that will-making was known in several states of Greece as early as the sixth century. It is probable that it existed in a rudimentary and oral form for some time before such legislation as that of Solon gave it formal recognition, but it is evident that it was not known in primitive times.[4] The ancient

[1] Plat. *Laws* 922 E: ΑΘ. μαλθακοὶ ἔμοιγ', ὦ Κλεινία, δοκοῦσιν οἱ πάλαι νομοθετοῦντες γεγονέναι καὶ ἐπὶ σμίκρον τῶν ἀνθρωπίνων πραγμάτων βλέποντές τε καὶ διανοούμενοι νομοθετεῖν.

ΚΛ. πῶς λέγεις;

ΑΘ. τὸν λόγον τοῦτον, ὦ 'γαθέ, φοβούμενοι τὸν νόμον ἐτίθεσαν τόνδε, ἐξεῖναι τὰ ἑαυτοῦ διατίθεσθαι ἁπλῶς ὅπως ἄν τις ἐθέλῃ τὸ παράπαν.

[2] Dem. 20. 102: ὁ μὲν Σόλων ἔθηκεν νόμον ἐξεῖναι δοῦναι τὰ ἑαυτοῦ ᾧ ἄν τις βούληται, ἐὰν μὴ παῖδες ὦσι γνήσιοι. *Id.* 46. 14: τὰ ἑαυτοῦ διαθέσθαι εἶναι ὅπως ἂν ἐθέλῃ, ἂν μὴ παῖδες ὦσι γνήσιοι ἄρρενες, ἂν μὴ μανιῶν ἢ γήρως ἢ φαρμάκων ἢ νόσου ἕνεκα, ἢ γυναικὶ πειθόμενος, ὑπὸ τούτων του παρανοῶν, ἢ ὑπ' ἀνάγκης ἢ ὑπὸ δεσμοῦ καταληφθείς. Cf. Dem. 44. 67; Isae. 6. 9; 2. 1; 9. 16, 17; Dem. 46. 16; 48. 56; Hyp. *Athenag.*, col. 8.

[3] Plut. *Sol.* 21.

[4] Cf. Maine, *Anc. Law*, pp. 193 ff., and Fustel de Coulanges, *La cité antique*, VII. 5, p. 87.

Hindoo legislation, which especially authorizes adoption when a man has no sons, knows nothing of the will in any form.[1] According to Plutarch, the law of Lycurgus did not recognize the will, and while Aristotle intimates that there was a free power of bequest in Sparta in his time, the fact that he assigns this as one of the chief causes of Sparta's ruin implies that it did not exist during all the five centuries of her prosperity that intervened between Lycurgus and his day. Plutarch tells us that the will was not permitted in Athens before the time of Solon. Aristotle speaks of a time when it was unknown in Corinth and Thebes.[2] The Cretan code of Gortyn, which dates from about the sixth century, knows nothing of the will, although it treats extensively of a highly developed form of adoption and intestate succession.[3]

We may then conclude that, while adoption was known in Greece from the earliest times, it is probable that will-making was not formally recognized till about the sixth century.

The sources for tracing the origin and development of the Greek will are very inadequate, and as a consequence writers on Greek law have usually contented themselves with taking it up at the time of the Attic orators, who afford a fertile field for the investigation of the subject. This is true not only of the will, but of Greek law in general. It is, in this respect, quite different from Roman law, for tracing the origin and development of which the sources are abundant. Hence it is that writers on the history of the will usually begin with the Roman, dismissing the Greek with a few desultory remarks. It is difficult, owing to the paucity of the sources, to trace with exactness the various steps in the evolution of Greek law from its earliest rudiments to the comparative complexity it had assumed at the time of the orators. But we are not left wholly to conjecture, for we find traces in the early poets of institutions and customs of the patriarchial period, and we have a few inscriptions that help to bridge over the gulf, although in some instances the exact significance of the terms used in these sources has not been determined.

Moreover, it is not easy to trace the development of the Greek will, although that development took place in the historical period; for until we come to the orators we have very little that is tangible outside of a few scattered, and not always very intelligible, inscriptions.[4]

[1] See *Laws of Manu*, 9. 104 ff.   [2] Arist. *Pol.* ii. 6, 12.

[3] *Law of Gortyn*, X, XI; cf. IV and V.

[4] Cf. Perrot., p. liii: "Nous n'avons sur la législation athénienne que des données bien incomplètes et bien fragmentaires; c'est donc à peine si, en ressemblant tous les

If we were to put implicit trust in the statements of the orators, we should believe that the final word with reference to wills, and in fact Greek law in general, was spoken by Solon; but this is evidently a professional device for working on the credulity of ignorant jurors; for it is easy to notice that when it suits their purpose they appeal to Solon, and when it does not they have no hesitation in ignoring his laws or quoting them to suit their argument.[1] Without doubt the laws of Solon were modified and added to between his time and that of the orators.[2]

Solon's laws, and especially those concerning inheritances, are often obscure; and this may have been intentional, with a view to giving greater power to the people as the interpreters of the law in the courts.[3] The dicasts took oath to give their decisions according to equity in absence of law.[4] A reflection of the power of the dicasts may be seen

textes, de quelque date qu'ils soient, nous n'arrivons à nous faire une juste idée de l'ensemble. Si nous prétendons traiter séparement l'œuvre législatif de Solon et celle de ces successeurs, nous n'avons plus que des détails qui ne s'assemblent et ne se rejoignent pas, qui souvent même se contredisent; toute vue générale nous est à peu pres interdite. Mieux vaut ne pas s'attarder à des distinctions où il est bien difficile de porter quelque rigueur, à des déterminations qui sont presque toujours purement conjecturales; mieux vaut se placer tout d'abord en face de législation athénienne, telle qu'elle existait dans le dernier siècle de la république entre le rétablissement de la démocratie par Thrasybule et la guerre lomiaque."

[1] Cf. Isae. 6. 28: οὐδὲ διαθέσθαι ἐᾷ ὅτῳ ἂν ὦσι παῖδες γνήσιοι with id. 10. 2: ὁ γὰρ νόμος κελεύει τὰ μὲν ἑαυτοῦ διαθέσθαι ὅτῳ ἂν ἐθέλῃ, τῶν δὲ ἀλλοτρίων οὐδένα κύριον πεποίηκε. In one case the clause "if there are no legitimate sons," suits his argument, and he misquotes the main clause in order to exaggerate its importance; in the other case it does not suit him and he omits it altogether. At one time the orators say, "A man can make any will he likes;" at another they say, "He can't make a will if ――――" Cf. Hyp. Athenag. Col. 8; Isae. 10. 22., etc.

[2] Cf. Beauchet, p. xlvi: "Les textes originaux des préscriptions soloniennes n'avaient point inspiré le respect séculaire qui entoura à Rome les règles de la loi des XII Tables. Leur autorité s'était affaiblie; le soin de leur conservation avait été négligé, et il est certain qu'ils étaient déjà sensiblement altérés à l'époque où Demosthène et orateurs ses rivaux s'en prévalaient en les attribuant à Solon."

[3] Cf. Aristot. Ἀθ. πολ. 9: ἔτι δὲ καὶ τὸ μὴ γεγράφθαι τοὺς νόμους ἀπλῶς μηδὲ σαφῶς, ἀλλ' ὥσπερ ὁ περὶ τῶν κλήρων καὶ ἐπικλήρων, ἀνάγκη πολλὰς ἀμφισβητήσεις γίνεσθαι καὶ πάντα βραβεύειν καὶ τὰ κοινὰ καὶ τὰ ἴδια τὸ δικαστήριον. Cf. Isae. 3. 68, 74, and Plut. Sol. 18.

[4] Dem. 20. 118: περὶ ὧν ἂν νόμοι μὴ ὦσι τῇ δικαιοτάτῃ κρινεῖν. Cf. Wyse, p. 176: "Solon committed the administration of justice to tribunals appointed by lot and invested with powers so ample that they became judges of equity as well as of law."

in *The Wasps* of Aristophanes, where one of them is represented as saying:

If a father when dying leaves an heiress daughter, assigning her to some husband, we tell the will and the case that sits so solemnly on its seals that it may go be hanged, for all we care, and we give her to whoever has won us over to his side by his persuasions. And this we do without fear of being called to account.[1]

The character of the Greek will at the time of the orators may be deduced from their writings, where, as has been intimated, the material for such deduction is comparatively plentiful; but if we would determine what the will was in its origin, it will be necessary to look further back into the past.

While, as has been stated, the direct sources for tracing the origin and development of the Greek will are inadequate, I think there is a point of attack that will yield a clear understanding of the subject. I refer to the ancient religious beliefs of the Greek people, traces of which are abundant in their literature, and out of which I believe most of their institutions grew.[2]

It is commonly accepted that the first human society or organization was the family, and that the earliest form of government was the patriarchal. Traces of this have existed up to our own time in the highlands of Scotland and in Russia—small communities consisting of several of our modern families living together under the leadership of a grandfather or great-grandfather. This was the case in prehistoric Greece. Homer, writing of the Cyclops, tells us that "they did not assemble for deliberation in the agora, nor for judicial decisions, but each had jurisdiction over his children and wives, and they did not trouble themselves about each other.[3] Plato asserts that men were originally under a patriarchal rule, such as is described by Homer in the above citation, and says: "This still remains in many places both

---

[1] Aristoph. *Vesp.* 583–87:

κἂν ἀποθνήσκων ὁ πατήρ τῳ δῶ καταλείπων παῖδ' ἐπίκληρον,
κλάειν ἡμεῖς μακρὰ τὴν κεφαλὴν εἴποντες τῇ διαθήκῃ
καὶ τῇ κόγχῃ τῇ πάνυ σεμνῶς τοῖς σημείοισιν ἐπούσῃ,
ἔδομεν ταύτην ὅστις ἂν ἡμᾶς ἀντιβολήσας ἀναπείσῃ,
καὶ ταῦτ' ἀνυπεύθυνοι δρῶμεν.

[2] Cf. Maine 190 ff., De Coulanges, *La cité antique*, pp. 4 and 7 ff.; Beauchet, pp. 13 f.

[3] *Odys.* 9. 112, 113: τοῖσιν δ' οὐ τ' ἀγοραὶ βουληφόραι οὔ τε θέμιστες . . . . θεμιστεύει δὲ ἕκαστος παίδων ἠδ ἀλόχων, οὐδ' ἀλλήλων ἀλέγουσιν. Cf. Hdt. 4. 106.

among Greeks and barbarians."[1]   Aristotle says that the most ancient
society could be called a family colony, for the individuals composing
it were ὁμογαλάκτες, παῖδές τε καὶ παίδων παῖδες.[2]

The most ancient people of Greece believed in the immortality of
the soul.   The soul, however, was not separated from the body at death,
but was buried with it and lived in the tomb underground.[3]   After
having buried the body, the mourners before departing called the
deceased by name, and said: "May the soil lie lightly above thee!"[4]
They had a great dread of the possibility of lack of burial.   If the
body was not buried, the soul had no dwelling-place, and became a
phantom restlessly roving over the earth and plaguing those whose
neglect to perform the burial rites had caused its misery.[5]

The dead thus continuing to exist under ground had need of food,
which it was the duty of their descendants to supply.   This was done
with regularity at set periods, and became a religious festival.[6]   These
ceremonies are described by Ovid and Vergil, in whose days they con-
tinued to exist, although they had become empty forms; for the most
cursory study of the religious beliefs of mankind will serve to show that
forms and ceremonies continue to be observed long after the beliefs
that gave them birth have become obsolete or mere superstitions. ⁻ The
tombs were decorated with flowers; cakes and fruits were placed on
them; milk, wine, and sometimes the blood of a victim were poured on
the ground over the body, and sometimes through a funnel leading to
the mouth of the body.[7]   Lucian, who, as Suidas tells us, was called
"The Blasphemer," says, in ridiculing these old beliefs:

It seems then that they are nourished by the libations and victims offered
by us upon their tombs; accordingly a dead person who has no friend or
relative left above ground is always in a famishing condition.[8]

[1] Plat. *Legg.* iii. 680 C.

[2] Aristot. *Politics* I. 2. 6.

[3] Eurip. *Alc.* 163.   Cf. Vergil describing the funeral of Polydorus: "We put to
rest the soul (*animam*) in the grave."   *Aen.* iii. 66 f.

[4] Verg. *Aen.* ii. 644, iii. 68; *Iliad* xxiii. 221; Eurip. *Alc.* 463; Pausan. ii. 7. 2.

[5] *Od.* xi. 72; Eurip. *Troad.* 1085; Hdt. 5. 92.

[6] See Ridgeway, *Early Age of Greece*, pp. 510 ff.; cf. Ridder, *L'Idée de la morte
en Grèce.*

[7] Verg. *Aen.* iii. 66, 67, 301; v. 77 f.; Ovid *Fast.* 535–42; cf. Hdt. 2. 40; Eurip. *Hec.*
536; *Iphig. I. T.* 162; Aesch. *Coeph.* 483–87 and Ridgeway, p. 510.

[8] Περὶ πένθους.

The care of the dead being thus obligatory upon their descendants, there grew up a religion of the dead in which they were regarded as gods.[1] Electra in her prayer to her dead father says:

I pray to thee that Orestes may come hither with some success and do thou hear me, father; and to myself grant that I may be far more chaste than my mother and more pious in action.[2]

This primitive religion was purely domestic. It was ancestor-worship. This is indicated by the word used by the Greeks to designate it.[3] The *Laws of Manu* represent the dead as repeatedly expressing the wish that sons may be born of their race who at regular intervals will give them rice boiled in milk, with honey and ghee.[4] It was considered a great crime for a son to fail to fulfil this obligation. As a consequence of these beliefs, it will appear that the perpetuation of the family was regarded as a sacred duty. Celibacy was impious, and the marriage became invalid if the wife proved barren.[5] "No man," says Isaeus, "knowing that he must die, is so careless of himself as to be willing to leave his family without descendants, for there would be no one to render him the worship that is due to the dead."[6] This duty could not be intrusted to a daughter, because when a daughter married she gave up her own ancestor's worship and adopted that of her husband. "From the hour of marriage the wife had no longer anything in common with the domestic religion of her fathers; she sacrificed at the hearth of her husband."[7]

When the natural means of procuring a son failed, in order that succession might remain unbroken the legal fiction of adoption was introduced. This seems to have been practiced as far back as we have any knowledge. The Hindoo law permitted a man who had no son by marriage to adopt one in order that the funeral rites

---

[1] Aesch. *Choeph.* 475–509; Soph. *Antig.* 451; Plut. *Sol.* 21; Plat. *Legg.* 927; Eurip. *Alc.* 1004.

[2] Aesch. *Choeph.* 138–41.   [3] πατριάζειν.

[4] *Laws of Manu* 3. 274. Cf. 9. 106, 107: "That son through whom the father pays his debt toward the manes and gains eternity is begotten for the sake of duty; the others they look upon as born of desire." The pregnant wife was called *djaha* because her husband was born again (*djahati*) in her (*ibid.* 9. 8). Cf. Jebb II, p. 316.

[5] *Laws of Manu* 9. 81. Cf. Hdt. 10. 39; 11. 61. Cf. Plut. *Sol.* 20.

[6] Isae. 7. 30.

[7] Stephanus of Byzantium, πάτρα.

might not cease."[1] "Adoption," says Isaeus, "is a right recognized by all men—Greeks and barbarians."[2] Again:

All those who see death approaching think of what will come after them, so as not to leave their house desolate, but to have someone to bring to their manes the necessary offerings, and to give to them the honors consecrated by custom. Wherefore, if they are about to die childless, they procure a son by adoption to leave behind them. And this is not only recognized by the individual, but also by the state, for by law it enjoins upon the archon the care of seeing that houses do not become desolate.[3]

In another speech he says:

Read to me the law which orders that a man be permitted to dispose of his property however he wishes, if there be no legitimate children; for the lawgiver, gentlemen of the jury, so made the law on this account, seeing that there was only this way of escape from desolation, this one consolation of life for all men, to be permitted to adopt whomever they wish.[4]

And in another place:

After this Menecles considers how he may not be childless, but have someone while living to take care of him, and when he died to bury him and for future time to perform the customary rites for him.[5]

If a man already had a son, the law did not permit him to adopt another;[6] for, as has been seen, the only reason for adoption was to prevent the family from becoming extinct; but if he had no sons and adopted one, and after the adoption a son was born to him, this did not take away the rights of the adopted son. Says Isaeus:

Now, in what sense was he "childless" who had left his nephew as his adopted son and heir, an heir to whom the law allows the succession just as to the issue of the body? The provision in the law is express that if a son is born to a man who has already adopted a son, both sons shall share alike in the inheritance.[7]

We have seen that the ancestor-gods which the Greeks worshiped had their abode in the grave where they were buried. They did not have common burial-places by the wayside, as in modern times, but each family (γένος) had originally its own burial-ground near the door.[8]

[1] *Laws of Manu*, 9. 141, 142, 159, 180. [2] Isae. 2. 21. [3] Isae. 7. 30. [4] Isae. 2. 13.

[5] Isae. 2. 10; cf. *ibid.* 46 and 7. 30: "That there may be someone to sacrifice to his manes and to perform the customary rites for him."

[6] Isae. 2. 11–14; Dem. 44 *passim;* cf. Beauchet II, p. 28.   [7] Isae. 6. 63.

[8] Eurip. *Hel.* 1163–68; Dem. 43. 79; *id.* 57. 28. Cf. de Coulanges, *Cité ant.*, p. 34, and authorities there cited: "Chaque famille avait son tombeau . . . . Tous ceux du même sang devaient y être enterrés et aucun homme d'une autre famille n'y pouvait être admis." Cf. also Ridder I, chap. 2.

It was thus necessary that a man should remain on the place where his ancestors were buried, in order to perform the sacred rites. From this naturally grew up the right of family possession of land. The family gods dwelt there; it was under their protection. A man had therefore no right to part with his land, for it belonged not to him, but to his family; and a family was a corporation, and corporations never die.[1] Hence we are not surprised to find that the ancient legislators in various states of Greece made laws forbidding the sale of one's patrimony and enjoining that the original allotments should remain unchangeable.[2]

From what has been said it will appear that the right to the land was transmitted in the same way as the right and duty to perform the religious rites, through sons only. A daughter could not inherit because she could not be intrusted with the celebrating of the family worship.[3] When a man left a daughter, but no sons, the difficulty was obviated by adopting a son and leaving him the estate on condition of his marrying the daughter. In such a case she was called an ἐπίκληρος — one on the estate, forming a part of it, as it were. She went with the estate to the heir.

This adoption was originally a solemn and public ceremony performed with the accompaniment of public assemblies, sacrifices, and oaths.[4] As the primary duty of the adopted son was to continue the family worship, it was natural that adoption was primarily a religious institution, and that the adopted son must be introduced into the sacred rites of the family of the adoptive father.[5] The first formality was his introduction into the phratry, or brotherhood of families, to which his adoptive father belonged. This took place at the regular meeting of the members of the phratry. The adoptive father presented a lamb or a goat for sacrifice. If the phratry refused to admit the person presented for adoption, the victim was removed from the altar.[6] The adoptive father led to the altar the person he desired to adopt and, placing his hand upon the altar, took oath that this person was born in lawful wedlock of a woman who was a citizen of the state. The members of the phratry then took oath to decide according to the laws, and, if the vote was favorable, the candidate was enrolled.[7]

[1] Cf. Maine, pp. 186 ff.
[2] Aristot. *Politics* ii. 6, 12; cf. ii. 7.   [3] See p. 48.
[4] Isae. 7. 14–17; cf. *Code of Gortyn*, X.
[5] ἐπὶ τὰ ἱερὰ ἄγειν (Isae. 7. 1).
[6] Isae. 7. 22; Dem. 43. 14; cf. Jebb II, p. 347, note.
[7] Dem. 43. 14.

The religious initiation of the candidate was not complete until he had also been introduced into the γένος[1] of the adoptive father, which was also a religious ceremony.[2] After this a third enrolment had to take place in the deme,[3] in order that he might be admitted to full political privileges.[4]

The son thus adopted was pledged to perform the duties of a son by marriage, and to fulfil all the obligations of his adoptive father, both divine and human.[5] Of course, he could not be adopted without his own consent, or, if he were a minor, the consent of his guardian was required.[6] The guardian could refuse to give his consent.[7]

Adoption among the Greeks was thus a solemn covenant. It was a contract, and could not be dissolved without the consent of both parties. Demosthenes tells us of a man who, having no son by marriage, adopted one and gave him his daughter with a certain portion. Afterward he quarreled with his adopted son, and took away the daughter and gave her to another man. The adopted son brought an action against him, and he "was compelled to meet all the demands that the adopted son brought against him." Then they came to a settlement on certain terms and "gave mutual releases from all demands."[8]

It is true that the law of Gortyn seems to show a weakening of the adopted son's claim. There the adoptive father appears to have had the right to put him away by making a public declaration before the assembled people, but even here his claim was recognized, for the adoptive father had to pay him ten staters by way of compensation.[9]

There were several good reasons why this public adoption should not suit in all cases. It probably often happened that a man did not wish to offend his other relatives and friends by the selection of one as his heir.[10] Anxiety to be on the safe side would lead a man to adopt a

[1] The original family, all of whose members were supposed to have been derived from a common ancestor.

[2] Isae. 7. 15: ἤγαγέ με ἐπὶ τοὺς βωμοὺς εἰς τοὺς γεννήτας τε καὶ φράτορας.

[3] The demes were political divisions established by Clisthenes (508 B. C.) on a democratic basis. The divisions were made by districts instead of by families, and aimed at breaking the power of the old aristocracy and admitting aliens to citizenship. Of course, previous to Clisthenes only the twofold registration in phratry and γένος was required.

[4] Dem. 44. 41, 44; cf. Isae. 7. 26–28, and see Jebb II. 327.

[5] Cf. Code of Gortyn, X.   [6] Isae. 7. 14.

[7] Isae. 2. 21: ἀλλ' οὐκ ἂν αὐτῷ ἔδωκεν, ἄπαιδα αὐτὸν καθιστάς.

[8] Dem. 41. 3–5.   [9] Code of Gortyn XI.

[10] Cf. Isae. 4. 13; cf. 9. 12: μηδένα ἐβούλετο εἰδέναι ὅτι τὸν Κλέωνος υἱὸν ἐποιεῖτο. Cf. id. 3. 72 and 4. 26; see also Wyse, p. 357.

son, sometimes when there was a possibility of his having sometime in the future a son born of his body,[1] especially if he were about to set out on a dangerous journey. If he should afterward have a son born to him, he could not, as we have seen, get rid of the one he had adopted. Again, the position of the adopted son was too sure during the life of the adoptive father to suit all cases. Even if he turned out to be disreputable and unworthy, or if the adoptive father quarreled with him, he could not revoke his decision.[2] There is no doubt that, in the ordinary course of human nature, it would not infrequently happen that the adopter would give a great deal to undo what he had done. These considerations led to putting off the adoption of a son as long as possible—in fact, till it was felt that death was imminent (*adoptio in extremis*), or the person was going to set out on a dangerous journey.[3]

Now, there was the serious objection to this course that an adoption could not be completed in a moment. The ceremonies required were too formal and extended, and they could be performed only at certain fixed times of the year.[4] A people of versatile genius, as quick of intuition and as little bound by formality and set laws as were the Greeks, naturally soon arrived at a solution of this problem. A man supposing himself to be in imminent danger of death, with the day for the assembling of the phratry several months distant, and facing the impossibility of making a complete adoption by the usual public ceremonies, called in his relatives and friends, and declared to them his choice of a person to continue his family worship and inherit his patrimony. The young man, of course, would be present (and, if there were time, would be initiated into the family worship), and would engage, either in his own person or in that of his guardian, to complete the adoption by the public registration ceremonies in the phratry and the deme after the death of the *de cuius*. These dispositions (διαθῆκαι) came to be committed to writing for greater exactness and to prevent misunderstanding; the document was called διαθήκη, and the *de cuius* was thus said διατίθεσθαι τὰ ἑαυτοῦ. This embryonic will-making was thus still public; and, if the *de cuius* did not die immediately, it had some of the serious

---

[1] Isaeus tells of a case where a man adopted the son of his sister by will (ἐν διαθήκῃ), on the condition that he should not have a son by his wife. Such an adoption could not have been made *inter vivos*, for adoption *inter vivos* was not revocable at will. Isae. 6. 5, 7; cf. Robiou, p. 63, and Beauchet II, p. 70.

[2] Dem. 41. 3–5.

[3] Cf. Isae. 7. 9; 6. 27; 9. 14, 15; 6. 5; 11. 8.

[4] Isae. 7. 5; cf. Meier-Schömann-Lipsius, p. 542; Beauchet, II, p. 12; Schulin, p. 17.

disadvantages, already mentioned, of the ordinary adoption *inter vivos*. Again, a man sometimes desired to make such provision when about to set out on a dangerous journey.[1] The natural desire for secrecy[2] caused him sometimes to refrain from communicating his intentions to the witnesses, and he merely declared to them that they were contained in a document which he sealed in their presence.[3] Thus the διαθήκη became secret.[4]

It is quite probable that Solon's law which permitted a man to dispose of his property as he pleased, if he had no legitimate male children born of his body, was intended to meet such a case as we have just described, and to make it formally legal.[5] The last clause seems to indicate that the purpose of the law was to provide a way for the continuance of the family, and this is in accord with what we have seen with respect to the early religious beliefs of the Greeks.

This "testamentary adoption" was not identical with adoption *inter vivos*, because the εἰσποίησις[6] was not legally complete. The term διατίθεσθαι came in to take the place of εἰσποιεῖσθαι, and the term διαθήκη for εἰσποίησις. It was a solemn setting-forth of the intentions of the *de cuius*, but the εἰσποίησις was not complete until the public ceremonies were gone through with after his death. This "testamentary adoption," for the reasons stated above, became the more popular, and we find that by the time of the orators it had almost driven out adoption *inter vivos*. It was not a complete legal contract like adoption *inter vivos*, but rather like an instrument drawn up and signed by one party and waiting for the signature of the other. The heir did not become legally a party to it until he had publicly signified his agreement by having himself enrolled in the phratry and the deme. As it was, of course, usually known that he would consent, and in fact he was most probably consulted beforehand,[7] it was regarded as a virtual εἰσποίησις, and often

[1]Cf. Soph. *Trach.* 155 ff.; Isaè. 6. 5, 27; 7. 9; 9. 14, 15; 11. 8.

[2]Isae. 6. 27; cf. 9. 12.

[3]Cf. Isae. 4. 13: ἔτι δὲ, ὦ ἄνδρες, καὶ τῶν διατιθεμένων, οἱ πολλοὶ οὐδὲ λέγουσι τοῖς παραγιγνομένοις ὅ τι διατίθενται, ἀλλ' αὐτοῦ μόνου, τοῦ καταλιπεῖν διαθήκας, μάρτυρας παρίστανται.

[4]On the relation between adoption and the Greek will, cf. Beauchet II, p. 19: "Il existe dans le droit attique, entre le testament et l'adoption un lieu étroit qu'on ne retrouve à un tel degré dans aucun autre législation."

[5]Cf. Dem. 44 *passim*.

[6]This word is used in Isae. 10. 14. The words ποίησις and θέσις are also used. ποιέω or εἰσποιέω with or without υἱόν signifies "to adopt."

[7]Cf. Dem. 41. 17; 18; 27. 43; 28. 14; and see chap. vi.

431

at first referred to as such,[1] and consequently was, in the eyes of the people of the time, a virtual contract or covenant.   Hence the word used to designate the act and the document.[2] ʹBut it must be remembered that it was not a contract in the eye of the law, and therefore there was nothing to prevent its revocation at the volition of the testator.[3]

Whatever interpretation may have been put upon Solon's law in the beginning, it is evident that soon it was not considered imperative that the son adopted by will should receive all of the estate.   Isaeus tells of a case where a man without sons adopted the son of a friend in a will, leaving to him only one-third of his estate.[4]   So in cases of testamentary adoption other bequests came to be made in the will, and while it is probable that Solon's law intended to permit will-making only to those who had not legitimate natural sons—and when it suits them the orators make a point on this interpretation[5]—yet we find that the common interpretation must have been rather that sons could not be disinherited;[6] for wills were made by men who had legitimate sons, and bequests to others sometimes amounting to more than half the property of the testator.[7]   Wills dividing up the property between the sons, giving one more than another, were made.[8]

It is not likely that it ever occurred to Solon that a man would want to bequeath his patrimony without adopting a son;[9] but such a restriction is not actually expressed in his law which gives a man liberty "to dispose of his own," and might easily be interpreted "to dispose of his own with full freedom."   At any rate, as time went on and the old religious belief in ancestor-worship began to die out, especially

---

[1] Cf. Isae. 3. 1, 42, 56, 57, 60, 61, 68, 69, 75, etc.   [2] See chap. iv.

[3] On this point see further chap. viii.   [4] Isae. 5. 6.   [5] Cf. Isae. 6. 28.

[6] Cf. Isae. 6. 44, where the statement is made that, if a man has legitimate sons, the law does not permit him to cast them off (ἐπανιέναι).

[7] Dem. 36. 8; 45. 28; 27. 4–5; Lys. 19. 39–45.   See chap. ix.

[8] Cf. Dem. 36. 34, 35.

[9] Cf. Robiou, pp. 67, 68: "Les principes du droit attique, les doctrines et les coutumes dont il découlait si directement, la foi à la religion domestique induisent à penser que jamais le législateur n'avait cru qu'il fût seulement possible de poser la question.   L'abandon de son patrimonie à une famille étrangère, sans la faire entrer dans la sienne, c'eut été la renonciation à toujours pour soi-même et pour ses ancêtres ceux libations funèbres qui devaient à la fois les honorer comme les dieux et les nourir comme des hommes, c'eut été le plus sacrilège des parricides, et si le vieux législateur d'Athènes a cru impossible le parricide matériel, ni lui ni aucun de ses contemporains n'avaient sans doute jamais prévu celui-là."

after the reforms of Clisthenes (508 B. c.), and the consequent weakening of the power of the γένος by the division of the people according to
locality instead of family, men would naturally chafe under the restriction. There seems to have been a protest against any restriction of
will-making power in Plato's time, and a belief in the right of absolute
individual ownership of property. In the *Laws* a man about to die is
represented as saying:

O ye gods how monstrous if I am not allowed to give or not to give
(bequeath) my own to whom I will—less to him who has been bad to me, and
more to him who has been good to me, and whose badness or goodness has
been tested by me in time of sickness or in old age and in every other kind
of fortune.[1]

As this sentiment grew, it is natural that the laws of Solon would be
interpreted more and more liberally. We have seen that men who had
sons made bequests, at the time of the orators, of a greater or less
amount, and men who were childless did not leave all of their property
to adopted sons. When the religious beliefs grew still weaker and at
last became obsolete toward the end of the fourth century and the
beginning of the third, we find, as we would expect, that the testament
became entirely independent of adoption. Its religious significance
disappeared, and people saw in it only a convenient means of regu-
lating the disposal of their property in view of death. At this point
the evolution of the will from adoption becomes complete.

[1] Plat. *Legg.* 922 C, D (Jowett).

CHAPTER VI

ITS FUNDAMENTAL CHARACTER

In the previous section I have endeavored to trace the origin and development of the Greek will. There remain some points connected with it that have long been matters of dispute, and so may warrant a separate treatment.

One of these questions is that of the legal character of the will. Some writers, claiming that it was a contract, have labored to account for the cases of seeming revocation at the volition of the testator; others concluding from these cases that it could not have been looked upon in such a light.

The word (διαθήκη) used to designate the Greek will, as we have seen in chap. iv, was also used to denote a solemn one-sided compact, or covenant. The Greeks themselves classed διαθῆκαι among συμβόλαια.[1] The word συμβόλαιον ordinarily means "contract," but can be used in a wide sense to denote "dealings between man and man."[2] There is an interesting case in this connection in the speech of Demosthenes against Spudias. He says:

> When Polyeuctus made this will, the defendant's wife was present, and of course she reported to him the will of her father, especially if he did not have an equal share, but it was to his disadvantage in all respects, and the defendant himself was invited to attend, so that he cannot say that it was a clandestine transaction and contrived behind their backs. When asked to come, he said he was engaged himself, but it would be sufficient for his wife to be there. Aristogenes gave him a full report of what had been done, and even then he made no remark about it; but, though Polyeuctus lived after that five days, he neither expressed any dissatisfaction when he went to the house nor made any remonstrance, nor did his wife, who was present at all of it from the beginning.[3]

Spudias, the defendant mentioned, was one of two testamentary co-heirs who had married the two daughters of Polyeuctus.

[1] Isae. 4. 12; 10. 10; Plato *Legg.* 913–22.
[2] For a fuller discussion of this word see chap. iv, pp. 34 f.
[3] Dem. 41. 17, 18.

In his first speech against Aphobus Demosthenes says:

But as to the legacy which was given to himself [Aphobus], though he admits that it was mentioned in the will, he says that he did not agree to it (ὁμολογῆσαι) in order that he may appear not to have received it.[1]

These citations seem to indicate that it was customary on making a will to consult the prospective heir and obtain his consent.

In Isaeus' speech concerning the estate of Philoctemon, as we have seen, we have a clear case of an instrument called διαθήκη that was a contract or covenant, and also served the purpose of a will.[2]

Contracts and wills were treated alike, at the time of the orators, with respect to the precautions taken to prevent fraud and the means for proving their authenticity. Witnesses were called at the making of both, and their names were recorded in the documents.[3] They were both sealed and deposited with persons who were held responsible for their safe-keeping.[4]

In a speech of Hypereides we have an illustration of how the Greeks classified wills. The speaker affirms that his written agreement (συνθήκη) with Athenogenes is invalid because of fraud and undue influence exerted upon him when it was made. He says:

Athenogenes will plead that the law declares that all agreements between man and man are binding.[5] Righteous (δίκαια) agreements, my dear sir. Unrighteous ones, on the contrary, it declares shall not be binding. . . . . One law forbids falsehood in the market-place; yet you have in open market made a contract with me to my detriment by means of falsehoods. . . . . There is a second law bearing on this point which relates to bargains between individuals by verbal agreements.[6] . . . . If a man shall give a woman in marriage justly and equitably (ἐπὶ δικαίοις), the children of such marriage shall be legitimate, but not if he betroths her on false representations and inequitable terms. Thus the law makes equitable marriages valid, but inequitable ones invalid. Again, the law relating to wills (τῶν διαθηκῶν) is of a similar nature. It enacts that a man may dispose of (διατίθεσθαι) his own property as he pleases, provided that he be not disqualified by old age or

[1] Dem. 27. 43; cf. 28. 14 ff.: "Says that he did not agree to any of the arrangements, but only heard Demophon reading a document and Therippides saying that the testator had made these dispositions."

[2] See chap. iv, § 4, where the citation is given in full.

[3] Isae. 9. 12; Dem. 35. 13; Diog. L. 5. 57. 74; *IJG* II, p. 62.

[4] Isae. 6. 7; 7. 1, 2; Dem. 32. 16; 33. 15, 35, 36; 34. 6; 35. 14; 48. 11; Isoc. 17. 20; Hyp. 5. 8, 9, 18; Diog. L. 4. 44; 5. 57. See Wyse, p. 386.

[5] ὡς ὁ νόμος λέγει ὅσα ἂν ἕτερος ἑτέρῳ ὁμολογήσῃ κύρια εἶναι.

[6] ὅσοι ὁμολογοῦντες ἀλλήλοις συμβάλλουσιν.

disease or insanity, or be influenced by a woman's persuasions, and that he be not in bonds or under any other constraint.   In circumstances, then, in which unrighteous wills relating solely to a man's own property are invalidated, how can it be right to maintain the validity of such an agreement as I have described which was drawn up by Athenogenes in order to steal property belonging to me.[1]   And if anyone under the persuasions of a woman writes a will (διαθήκας) for the arrangement of his property, shall it be invalid, while, if I am persuaded by Athenogenes' mistress and entrapped into making this agreement (ταῦτα συνθέσθαι), I must be ruined in spite of the express support which is given me by law?   Can you dare to rely on the contract (συνθήκαις) of which you and your mistress secured the signature by fraud?[2]

In this connection the analogy of the ancient Roman will may be instructive, especially in view of the fact that it has been recently demonstrated that Greek law was one of the chief sources of Roman law,[3] or that they were derived from a common source and followed a similar course of development.[4]   It is asserted by several ancient authorities that the Romans sent a delegation to Greece to get materials for the preparation of the famous code of the Twelve Tables.[5]

The ancient Roman plebeian will— *Testamentum per aes et libram* — had its origin in the *mancipium* and required a solemn and intricate ceremonial.[6]   It was a conveyance *inter vivos*.   The heir was called *familiae emptor*, purchaser of the estate (*familia*).   The transaction required the presence of a scale-holder (*libripens*) with a pair of scales to weigh the copper money.   This became later a symbolical ceremony.[7]

We have seen that the adoption out of which the Greek will developed was a solemn covenant publicly instituted with religious ceremonies.   Although in case of adoption by will the act was not completed in the will itself—not until the heir had himself enrolled in the

[1] ὅπου δὲ οὐδὲ [περὶ] τῶν αὑτοῦ ἰδίων αἱ [μὴ δ]ίκαιαι διαθῆκαι κύριαί εἰσιν, πῶς Αθηνογ[έ]νει γε κα[τὰ τῶ]ν ἐμῶν συνθεμέν[ων τ]οιαῦτα δεῖ κύρια εἶναι.

[2] Hyp. 5. 13 ff.; Kenyon, pp. 17 ff.   I have used Kenyon's translation in the main, taking the liberty of altering it to make it more literal in a few sentences, and to suit Blass's text, which I have preferred in one instance.

[3] By Hofmann, *Griechisches und römisches Recht*, pp. 1 ff.; cf. Beauchet I, pp. xxii–xxvii; Gide, p. 85; Reinach in *Nouvelle revue historique du droit*, 1893, p. 14.

[4] de Coulanges, *Cité ant.*, p. 1.

[5] Livy (iii. 31) says that before the code was drawn up "missi legati Athenas . . . . iussique inclitas leges Solonis describere, et aliarum Graeciae civitatum mores iuraque noscere."

[6] The ceremony is described by Gaius ii. 104; cf. iii. 173, 174.

[7] The evolution of the will from this source is traced at length by Maine, pp. 203 ff.

phratry and the deme after the death of the testator—yet, as it was understood that this would follow as a matter of course, it was natural that in its origin the will should be looked upon in the same light as the institution whose place it was incipiently taking and whose functions it was fulfilling.   This accounts for the fact that the people classed it among contracts, and used a word to designate it which signified a solemn one-sided covenant.[1]

[1] See chap. iv.   It is a significant fact that the earliest author in whose writings this word is found uses it clearly in both senses—"covenant" and "will."   See Aristoph. *Av.* 440; *Vesp.* 584, 589.

CHAPTER VII

MAKING AND SAFE-KEEPING

The ceremony of will-making was at first no doubt elaborate and formal, requiring the presence of the archon as well as of members of the γένος, phratry, and deme;[1] but as the will became more and more independent of the old religious beliefs, these formalities were dispensed with at the discretion of the testator. At the time of the orators usually a large number of witnesses were called in, consisting of the testator's relatives, phratores, demesmen, and friends.[2] In their presence the testator designated a document as his will, and sealed it.[3] When a man desired to avoid publicity, he called in few witnesses. The father of Demosthenes called only one besides the three men whom he appointed guardians of his children.[4] In fact, when a man did not want it known that he was making a will, he could dispense with witnesses altogether, although, for obvious reasons, it is not probable that this was often done.[5]

The names of the witnesses were written in the document,[6] but they did not affix their signatures to it; for Isaeus says that they could only testify to the fact that a will had been made by the testator, and not that the will produced in court was the same as that which they had been called to witness.[7] It seems not to have been necessary even that

[1] de Coulanges, *Nouvelles recherches*, p. 36.

[2] Isae. 9. 8: μὴ ἄνευ τῶν οἰκείων τῶν ἑαυτοῦ τὰς διαθήκας ποιεῖσθαι· ἀλλὰ πρῶτον μὲν συγγενεῖς παρακαλέσαντα, ἔπειτα δὲ φράτορες καὶ δημότας τῶν ἄλλων ἐπιτηδείων ὅσους δύναιτο πλείστους· οὕτω γὰρ εἴτε κατὰ γένος εἴτε κατὰ δόσιν ἀμφισβητοίη τις, ῥᾳδίως ἂν ἐλέγχοιτο ψευδόμενος.

[3] Isae. 7. 1: διέθετο τὴν οὐσίαν ἑτέρῳ, καὶ ταῦτ' ἐν γράμμασι κατέθετο παρά τισι σημηνάμενος.

[4] Dem. 28. 15.

[5] Isae. 9. 9–12. In § 12 he says: εἰ μὲν ὁ Ἀστύφιλος μηδένα ἐβούλετο εἰδέναι ὅτι τὸν Κλέωνος υἱὸν ἐποιεῖτο, μηδ' ὅτι διαθήκας καταλίποι, εἰκὸς ἦν μηδὲ ἄλλον μηδένα ἐγγεγράφθαι ἐν τῷ γραμματείῳ μάρτυρα· εἰ δ' ἐναντίον μαρτύρων φαίνεται διαθέμενος, ... Cf. Meier-Schömann-Lipsius, p. 695, n. 299; Schulin, p. 8; Caillemer in *Annuaire*, p. 173; Beauchet III, p. 658; and Wyse, p. 634.

[6] Isae. 9. 12; Diog. Laert. 5. 57, 74; cf. Beauchet III, p. 659.

[7] Isae. 4. 12, 14. He overlooks, probably "with malice aforethought," the fact that they could identify it by means of the testator's seal, but he would not have been able to use such an argument if the witnesses usually had signed the will.

the document be written by the testator himself, or that he should affix his own signature to it.[1]

This mode of making a will provided no adequate protection against forgery, as it is evident that the document might be changed altogether or in part by anyone who could get access to it.[2] Accordingly, sometimes the testator read the document to the witnesses, but, on account of the usual desire for secrecy, this was seldom done.

The usual method of safeguard was the affixing of the testator's seal to the will.[3] This took the place of his signature, and served as a positive means of identification.[4]

The will thus made and sealed was usually deposited with some trustworthy person (or persons, if more than one copy were made) for safe-keeping.[5] This person might be a relative or friend of the testator. Isaeus tells us of a will that was deposited with an uncle;[6] of another deposited with a brother-in-law;[7] of another, with a relative (προσήκων).[8] Referring to the depositing of wills in general he uses the expression "with certain persons."[5] Demosthenes uses a similar expression.[9]

Sometimes as a further safeguard several copies (ἀντίγραφα) were made and deposited with different persons. There were three copies of the will of Theophrastus "sealed with the ring of Theophrastus." These were deposited with three different persons, who are named, and each deposit was made in the presence of four witnesses, whose names are set down in the will. These seem to be private citizens, friends of the testator. There were three copies also of the will of Arcesilaus, Theophrastus' pupil and founder of the Middle Academy, which were deposited in three different cities with three friends.[10]

We find only two instances in which a will was deposited in official custody: one mentioned by Isaeus, where it was deposited with one of the astynomoi;[11] and one in an inscription from Amorgos, where it was

---

[1] M.-S.-L., p. 595; Beauchet III, 660; Schulin, pp. 7, 8. [2] Isae. 4. 12, 13.

[3] Isae. 7. 1, 2; Dem. 45. 17; Diog. Laert. 5. 57; Aristoph. *Vesp.* 585 ff.

[4] Perrot, *Éloquense politique*, p. 372.

[5] Isae. 7. 1 (where he is speaking of wills in general): κατέθετο παρά τισι.

[6] Isae. 9. 5; cf. 9. 6 and 9. 18.

[7] Isae. 6. 7: καὶ τὴν διαθήκην κατέθετο παρὰ τῷ καδεστῇ Χαιρέᾳ, τῷ τὴν ἑτέραν αὐτοῦ ἀδελφὴν ἔχοντι.

[8] Isae. 6. 27. [9] Dem. 36. 7: παρ' οἶς αἱ διαθῆκαι κεῖνται. [10] Diog. L. 5. 57; 4. 44.

[11] Isae. 3. 14, 15, 18, 25. Cf. Wyse, p. 194: "No other example is known of State officials taking charge of a will in which the State had no interest." Accordingly, he thinks this may have had some connection with State affairs.

deposited in three copies "in the temple of Aphrodite, and with the archon Eumonides, and with the thesmothete Ctesiphon.' This will contained a legacy in favor of the goddess, and this probably accounts for its official depositing.

There is no evidence or trace of registration of Greek wills in the classic period, nor of official inspection of their contents.[2]

[1] *CIG* 2264 *u; IJG* I. 110, n. 24.

[2] "The registration of wills in Ptolmaic Egypt (Mahaffy, *Flinders Petrie Papyri*, I, nn. 11–21) was a consequence of the Egyptian succession duty." Wyse, p. 194; cf. Ramsay, pp. 354 f.

CHAPTER VIII

CODICILS, MODIFICATION, REVOCATION

If at any time after a man had written his will he wished to add something to it or to correct it, it is obvious that, if he had not deposited it nor communicated its contents to witnesess, he could do so at pleasure. If he had deposited it, and could get it back from the depositee, the same would be true. If, however, he could not get it back from the depositee in time, he could write additional clauses (προσγράψαι) in another document (γραμματεῖον).[1] He was at liberty also to demand it back from the depositee for the purpose of making corrections (ἐπανορθῶσαι).[2]

We have seen that the adoption from which the Greek will was derived was a legal contract which could not be revoked without the consent of both parties to it. This, together with the facts with respect to its fundamental nature discussed in chap. vi, has given rise to the idea that it was also a contract, and consequently irrevocable. But, as has been shown, since even in its rudimentary stage of testamentary adoption the εἰσποίησις was not completed by the will itself, it was not a contract in the eye of the law, and consequently, while adoption *inter vivos* was irrevocable except by the consent of both parties, testamentary adoption could be revoked at the pleasure of the testator.

Obviously, if the contents of the will had not been communicated to witnesses, as long as the testator kept it in his own possession he could revoke it by the substitution of another document, or by simply destroying it and dying intestate. If, however, he had deposited it for safe-keeping as indicated above, it seems to have been the custom to demand it back from the depositee in order to destroy it. This would probably be done in the presence of a magistrate and witnesses (preferably the original witnesses to the will). Isaeus tells of a man who, having quarreled with the guardian of his intestate heirs—his nephews

[1] Isae. I. 25: εἴ τι προσγράψαι τούτοις ἐβούλετο, διὰ τί οὐκ ἐν ἑτέρῳ γράψας γραμματείῳ κατέλιπεν, ἐπειδὴ τὰ γράμματα παρὰ τῶν ἀρχόντων οὐκ ἐδυνήθη λαβεῖν; If codicils were not permitted, such a question would have been absurd in the mouth of the most sophistical lawyer and before the most ignorant judges. Continuing he says: γράψαι δ' ἐξῆν εἰς ἕτερον εἴ τι ἐβούλετο, καὶ μηδὲ τοῦθ' ἡμῖν ἀμφισβητήσιμον ἐᾷν. Cf. Meier-Schömann-Lipsius, p. 597; Schulin, p. 9; Beauchet III, p. 668; Guiraud, p. 253; Hille, p. 76.

[2] Isae. I. 26.

—made a will in favor of several more distant relatives. Just before his death he sent for the magistrate (ἀστύνομος) who had charge of it, but one of the legatees refused to admit him. The testator became angry and ordered the magistrate to be summoned for the next day, but died that night without having seen him. The nephews now claimed that their uncle had virtually revoked his will, because he had sent for the magistrate for the purpose of revoking (λῦσαι, ἀνελεῖν) it; and the legatees claimed that he had sent for him in order to make corrections (ἐπανορθῶσαι) in it and to confirm (βεβαιῶσαι) the bequest to themselves. As both of these are treated as valid suppositions, whatever may have been the testator's intentions, we may conclude that a will could be legally revoked or revised in the manner indicated.[1]

The only instance we have of the refusal of a depositee to deliver over a διαθήκη at the demand of the διαθέμενος is explained by the fact that the document in question was a contract as well as a will.[2] The depositee, when summoned to produce it in court, refused to give it up for revocation without the consent of all the contracting parties. The διαθέμενος obtained the consent of all the parties to the διαθήκη that were present, but the depositee still refused to give it up until a guardian should be appointed to act for the daughter of one of the depositors who was now deceased. In this he was sustained by the archon. The διαθέμενος then made an agreement of some kind, which is not specified, before the archon and the assessors and many witnesses, to the effect that the διαθήκη was no longer binding upon him.[3] This was the regu-

---

[1] Isae. I. 3: The defendants rely on a will which he made in anger and annulled (ἔλυσε) before his death, having sent Poseidippus for the magistrate.

Ibid. 14: When he was suffering from the illness from which he died, he desired to revoke (ἀνελεῖν) this will, and charged Poseidippus to bring in the magistrate.

Ibid. 18: They rely on the will, asserting that Cleonymus sent for the magistrate, not because he wished to annul (λῦσαι) it; but to correct (ἐπανορθῶσαι) it and to confirm (βεβαιῶσαι) the legacy (δωρεάν) to themselves. Now it is for you to consider, whether, when Cleonymus became friendly to us, he desired to revoke (ἀνελεῖν) the will made in anger, or to take measures how he should more surely deprive us of his property.

Ibid. 21: If he sent for the magistrate because he wished to revoke (ἀνελεῖν) the will, as we affirm, there is not a word for them to say.

Ibid. 25: For it was not possible to revoke (ἀνελεῖν) any other document than the one deposited with the magistrate.

Ibid. 42: The defendants prevented him from revoking (ἀνελεῖν) the will when he wished to do so.

Ibid. 43: Cleonymus annulled (ἔλυσε) the will when in his right mind, but he made (διέθετο) it in anger.

Ibid. 50: He was right in determining to annul (λῦσαι) the will.

[2] Isae. 6. 31–33. See chap. iv, § 4.

[3] διομολογησάμενος ἐναντίον τοῦ ἄρχοντος καὶ τῶν παρέδρων καὶ ποιησάμενος πολλοὺς μάρτυρας ὡς οὐκέτ᾿ αὐτῷ κέοιτο ἡ διαθήκη.

lar method of procedure when a man wished legally to free himself from the obligation of a contract, when he had what he considered legitimate reasons for so doing.[1] In the case just mentioned a settlement seems to have been arrived at before the archon and assessors, and soon after we find the διαθέμενος acting in such a manner as to indicate that this mode of procedure was regarded as effective (§ 33).[2]

It does not seem that the practice of canceling an earlier will by a later prevailed at Athens.[3] We find, however, what appears to be an example of this custom in an inscription from Tegea referred to above.[4]

[1] See Dem. 48. 46, 47: ἐχρῆν γὰρ αὐτόν, εἴ τι ἀληθὲς ἦν ὧν λέγει, ... παραλαβόντα πολλοὺς μάρτυρας ἀξιοῦν ἀναιρεῖσθαι τὰς συνθήκας παρὰ τοῦ Ἀνδροκλείδου, ὡς παραβαίνοντος ἐμοῦ καὶ τἀναντία πράττοντος ἐαυτῷ καὶ οὐκέτι κυρίων οὐσῶν τῶν συνθηκῶν ἐμοὶ καὶ τούτῳ, καὶ τῷ Ἀνδροκλείδῃ τῷ ἔχοντι τὰς συνθήκας διαμαρτύρασθαι, ὅτι αὐτῷ οὐδέν ἐστιν ἔτι πρᾶγμα πρὸς τὰς συνθήκας ταύτας.

[2] Authorities on Greek law, while generally recognizing the fact that the διαθήκη in question must have been essentially a contract, have invariably referred to it as an example of the revocation of a "testament," in case the testator could not recover it from the depositee. The reference is not to the point when treating of a "mere will," unless regarded as an argument a fortiori. Cf. Meir-Schömann-Lipsius, pp. 597, 598; Schulin, p. 9; Guiraud, p. 253; Hille, pp. 76 ff.; Beauchet III, pp. 669–72.

[3] If in the speech of Isaeus concerning the inheritance of Cleonymus the nephews were right in affirming that the purpose of sending for the will was to revoke it, it would seem that we might conclude that the Attic law did not permit the liberty of canceling an earlier will by a later; but if he wished merely to modify it, this would not be so evident. As the orator produces proof of his being at variance with only one of the legatees (Pherenicus), he may have desired to modify his dispositions with reference to him only. He may have had still other reasons for its recall. The sentence generally cited in proof of the opinion that a will could not be revoked without getting it back from the depositee (Isae. I. 25: ἀνελεῖν . . . . οὐχ οἷός τ' ἦν ἄλλο γραμματεῖον ἢ τὸ παρὰ τῇ ἀρχῇ κείμενον) is such a peculiar statement as to awaken suspicion either that the text has been corrupted in transmission, or that the orator was intentionally obscure at this point.

Wyse asks: "If the former dispositions of a testator could be altered in a supplement, what prevented the use of a 'codicil' as an instrument to revoke a prior will?" It is quite probable that corrections might practically revoke the original will, and to this there seems to be no serious objection. The custom of demanding the will back from the depositee for the purpose of destroying it, instead of making a new one, was probably due to the fact that they had not yet caught the idea that came to the Romans later. Even the simplest, and after they are known apparently self-evident, ideas are often slow in coming to the mind.

Since writing the above, I have noticed a good brief discussion of this point in an article in Hermathena XXXII (1906), by W. A. Goligher, M.A.: "Isaeus and Attic Law."

[4] See pp. 41, 42.

CHAPTER IX

LIMITATION BY THE EXISTENCE OF SONS

A very interesting question with reference to Greek wills, and one that has been the source of much argument, is whether a man who had legitimate sons could make a valid will; and, if so, under what limitations, if any. The answer to this question has already been given in brief in the chapter on origin and development, but because of the importance I will now discuss it more fully.

Solon's law which says that a man "can bequeath his property as he pleases if he have not legitimate male children" does not mean, as it has been sometimes interpreted, that a man with legitimate sons cannot make a will. It seems to me that the most that can be deduced from it is that, if a man have legitimate sons, he cannot make whatever kind of will he pleases—his power of testation is restricted; he must take his sons into account.

It should be noticed also that, when quoting Solon's law concerning wills, the orators do not always put in the clause "if there be no legitimate sons." As has been intimated before, Isaeus omits it when it does not suit his argument. It is still more significant that Hypereides, who quotes this law with minuteness in all the other details, omits this clause altogether—and this in a case in which its insertion would not be detrimental to his argument.[1] Aristotle also, when quoting this law in his *Athenian Constitution*, makes no reference to the clause in question, and says that the Thirty "made the testator absolutely (καθάπαξ) free to dispose of his property as he pleased."[2] Plato says that the ancient legislators allowed a man to dispose of his property by will in all respects "as he pleased," and makes no mention of the limiting clause in question.[3]

However these citations may be explained, it is indisputable that at the time of the orators men with legitimate sons could and did make valid wills.

[1] For the complete citation see pp. 57, 58.

[2] Ἀθ. πολ. 35: περὶ τοῦ δοῦναι τὰ ἑαυτοῦ ᾧ ἂν ἐθέλῃ κύριον ποιήσαντες καθάπαξ τὰς δὲ προσούσας δυσκολίας, ἐὰν μὴ μανιῶν ἢ γήρως ἕνεκα ἢ γυναικὶ πειθόμενος, ἀφεῖλον.

[3] See p. 43.

[444

Demosthenes tells of a banker named Pasion who had two sons, and who made a will dividing the bulk of his estate unequally between them.[1] He left to his wife a legacy of two talents, a lodging-house worth two hundred minas, and female slaves and household property.[2] Lysias tells us of a man who had two sóns and a daughter, and who left a will bequeathing one talent and the household stuff to his wife, and one talent to his daughter, and the remainder to his sons.[3] He tells us also of another man who in his will bequeathed to Apollo and Diana sixteen talents and forty minas; to a brother, three talents; and to his only son, the remainder, consisting of seventeen talents, less than half of his estate.[4] The father of Demosthenes in his will bequeathed to Therippides, who was no relation to him, the income from seventy minas till his son should come of age; to Demophon, a nephew, his daughter with a portion of two talents; and to Aphobus, another nephew, his widow with a portion of eighty minas, and the use of his house and furniture; and the rest of his property to his only son.[5]

In an inscription from Erythrae (Ionia) of about the middle of the third century we learn of a man with two sons who left a will dividing his property between them and his wife.[6]

At Sparta in the fourth century, according to Plutarch, by the law of Epitadeus a man was free to dispose of his property by will as he pleased, even if he had sons.[7]

Polybius tells us that in Boeotia toward the end of the third century many men who had children bequeathed the greater part of their property for the maintenance of feasts and convivial entertainments.[8]

There seems to have been no specified restriction on the part of an estate that could be bequeathed away from the sons. It was rather, like many other things in Greek law, left to custom, and to the decisions of the courts in cases of dispute. Demosthenes argues that the fact that his father had left four and a half talents in doweries and legacies was a presumption in favor of his reckoning the total value of the estate at about fourteen talents, "for," says he, "it could not be supposed that he would desire to leave me, his son, in poverty, and to heap riches upon these men who were rich enough already.[9] He seems to argue

[1] Dem. 36. 8, 34.

[2] Dem. 45. 28.

[3] Lys. 32. 5, 6.

[4] Lys. 19. 39–41.

[5] Dem. 27. 4, 5.

[6] Dittenberger 600.

[7] Plut. *Agis.* 5.   See p. 42.

[8] Polyb. xx. 6.

[9] Dem. 29. 44.

here only from probability (having already arrived at the total of four-teen talents in another manner), and to admit the possibility of a father's leaving his son in poverty and enriching other men.

We have seen that Lysias gives an example of a will in which more than half was bequeathed away from the son; that among the Boeotians "the greater part" could be bequeathed away from the family; and that, in Sparta, a man could disinherit his son altogether by will.

CHAPTER X

RELATION TO ADOPTION

Could a valid Greek will be made without adoption? Perhaps there has been more misunderstanding on this question than on any other point connected with Greek wills, the difficulty arising, as in other cases, from overlooking the fact of the development of Greek law in consequence of the changing of the old religious beliefs. The answer depends on the time to which reference is made. As we have noticed in tracing the origin and development of the Greek will, the chief stages were first adoption *inter vivos*, then testamentary adoption, then wills adopting a son and making bequests to others, and finally wills entirely divorced from adoption. It is, of course, impossible to draw strict lines of demarkation at definite periods.

The text of Solon's law which says that a man "may bequeath his own as he will if there be no legitimate sons born of his body" (ἐξεῖναι τὰ ἑαυτοῦ διαθέσθαι ἐὰν μὴ παῖδες ὦσι γνήσιοι ἄρρενες, κτλ.) would seem to give absolute liberty of testation to those who had no legitimate sons. To escape this interpretation it is sometimes claimed that διαθέσθαι is equivalent to εἰσποιεῖσθαι or ποιεῖσθαι. Some color is given to this claim by the fact that a majority of the cases of will-making mentioned in the orators include adoption, and in some instances the person adopted is made universal heir. In this last case, of course, the terms are mutually inclusive, but the orators do not use them as equivalent.[1]

That the terms in question are not equivalent is shown conclusively by the fact that διατίθεσθαι (also διαθήκη) is used of wills which do not

[1] Cf. Isae. 6. 53: "How do you know that Philoctemon *neither made a will nor adopted* Chaerestratus as his son?" (οὔτε διέθετο οὔτε υἱὸν Χαιρέστρατον ἐποιήσατο). Here the terms διέθετο and υἱὸν ἐποιήσατο seem to be mutually exclusive. This is shown by the use of οὔτε . ּ . . οὔτε instead of using a participial construction, or at least καί.

Dem. 44. 65: "If the deceased *had adopted* anyone, we would have agreed to it; or if he *had left a will*, we would have stood by it" (εἰ μὲν ὁ τελευτηκὼς ἐποιήσατό τινα συνεχωροῦμεν ἂν αὐτῷ, ἢ εἰ διαθήκας καταλελοίπει, καὶ ταύταις ἂν ἐνεμείναμεν).

Isae. 9. 7: "If he had intended to leave a son by adoption" (υἱὸν ποιησάμενον καταλιπεῖν). Why use this circumlocution, if διατίθεσθαι meant the same thing?

Ibid. 9. 1: ὡς οὔτε ἐποιήσατε ἐκεῖνος υἱὸν ἑαυτῷ οὔτε ἔδοκε τὰ ἑαυτοῦ, οὔτε διαθήκας κατέλιπεν. If the terms in question were synonymous, surely the first clause is an unwarranted superfluity.

Cf. 3. 42, 68; 9. 34, 35; Beauchet III, p. 696; Wyse 326.

contain any adoption, and where in fact no adoption was possible
because the testator had legitimate sons; for example, the will of the
father of Demosthenes, of Pasion, of Conon, of Diodotus, and of others
mentioned in the previous chapters.[1]

These just referred to are examples of valid wills which do not
include any adoption where the testator had one or more sons. Wills
were made also bequeathing all of the estate without adoption when the
testator was childless. To this class probably belongs the will of
Cleonymus, mentioned by Isaeus. Cleonymus died childless, and
bequeathed his estate away from the intestate heirs, his nephews, to
several remote kinsmen—Poseidippus, Diocles, and Pherenicus and
his brothers. There is no mention or hint of adoption. The fact that
there are several heirs by the will who seem to share equally, as well as
the word that is used to designate the inheritance,[2] speaks against any
idea of adoption. He would not, of course, adopt them all, and no
one of them seems to be singled out.

Another example from Isaeus of such a will seems to be the case in
which Eupolis claimed to have been made universal heir to the estate
of his brother Mneson,[3] in the speech concerning the inheritance of
Apollodorus. There are several other instances in the orators in which
no reference is made to adoption, and it cannot be determined whether
any such thing was included in the will or not.

The wills of the philosophers, Theophrastus,[4] Straton,[5] Lycon,[6] and
Epicurus,[7] dating from the third century have been preserved for us
entire.[8] In all of these the whole estate of the testator is distributed
in various legacies; details are given with reference to various matters,
such as the burial of the testator, enfranchisement of favorite slaves,
appointment of executors, etc.; but none of them contains any
adoption.[9]

[1] Dem. 27. 4, 5; 36. 8, 34; Lys. 19. 39–41; 32. 5, 6.

[2] Isae. 1. 18. The beneficiaries under the will claimed that Cleonymus had sent
for his will ἐπανορθῶσαι καὶ βεβαιῶσαι σφίσι αὐτοῖς τὴν δωρεάν. Δωρεά is a *bequest*. A
son or an adopted son would refer to his inheritance as κλῆρον. Cf. Schulin, p. 22;
Beauchet III, p. 695.

[3] Isae. 7. 6.   [4] Diog. Laert. 5. 51.   [5] 5. 61.   [6] 5. 69.   [7] 10. 16.

[8] There is no doubt as to the authenticity of these documents. See Dareste in
Annuaire, 1882, p. 1. As Theophrastus was a juvisconsult of ability, the author of
several works on jurisprudence, his testament should be of special importance from a
legal standpoint.

[9] These wills have been edited and annotated by Bruns in the *Zeitschrift der
Savigny-Stiftung für Rechtsgeschichte*, Vol. I, "Romanistische Abtheilung," 1, pp. 1–
53; and by Dareste in *Annuaire des études grecques*, Vol. XVI; cf. Schulin, pp. 32 ff.

In a Doric inscription will dating from the fifth century there is no adoption, and a woman is made universal heir.[1]

In an inscription from Dodona (in Epirus) dating from the fourth century a man leaves all his property to a corporation.[2]

In a long and complete inscription will of the second century a certain Alcesippus of Colydon (Delphi) makes a testamentary foundation of a definite amount and bequeaths all the rest of his estate to the city of Delphi, deducting the expense of his funeral.[3]

I have not found any example of adoption in any of the inscription wills, nor in any of the inscriptions in which wills are mentioned.[4]

As has been seen, the law of Epitadeus made testation absolutely free in Sparta in the fourth century.[5]

Aristotle says that the Thirty gave a man absolute liberty to bequeath his property as he pleased.

Adoption was not necessary to will-making in Boeotia in the third century. Men without children often bequeathed all their property for the maintenance of feasts, and many even of those who had children bequeathed the greater part of their estates for a like purpose.[6]

In the time of Isaeus at Athens a woman could not make a valid will,[7] but we find examples of wills made by women, dating from the end of the third and the beginning of the second centuries.[8]

We may then conclude that at the time of the orators a man could dispose of his property by will without adoption; that wills not including adoption were perhaps unusual at that time, but became more and more common until, in the third century, the will came to be entirely divorced from the idea of adoption that had given it birth.

---

[1] *CIG* 4. See p. 40.

[2] Rhangabé, *Archäol. Zeitung* XXXVI. 116; *IJG*, 2d ser. I, p. 61.

[3] *IJG*, 2d ser. 1, p. 62.

[4] Cauer, Nos. 10 and 123; Dittenberger 600; *Bull. corr. hell.* X, 18, p. 381; Collitz *Dialectinschr.* III. 3380 and 3634; *CIG* 1850, 2264 *u*, 2448, 2690, 3142, 3394, 3631, 3847 *p*, 3953 *b*, 4303 *h*.

[5] The ephor had the law passed for the express purpose of disinheriting his son, with whom he had quarreled.

[6] Polyb. xx. 6: οἱ μὲν γὰρ ἄτεκνοι τὰς οὐσίας οὐ τοῖς κατὰ γένος ἐπιγενομένοις τελευτῶντες ἀπέλειπον, ὅπερ ἦν ἔθος παρ' αὐτοῖς πρότερον, ἀλλ' εἰς εὐωχίας καὶ μέθας διετίθεντο, καὶ κοινὰς τοῖς φίλοις ἐποίουν. πολλοὶ δὲ καὶ τῶν ἐχόντων γενεὰς ἀπεμέριζον τοῖς συσσιτίοις τὸ πλεῖον μέρος τῆς οὐσίας.

[7] Isae. 10. 10.

[8] E. g., *CIG* 2448, the long and complete "testament of Epicteta," and Cauer (1st ed.), No. 19, the will of "Agasicrates' daughter Tisias." Cf. Schulin, pp. 42 ff., who edits several wills of this class.